What is

PROCESS
THOUGHT?

What is

PROCESS

THOUGHT?

SEVEN ANSWERS TO SEVEN QUESTIONS

Jay McDaniel

PROCESS
CENTURY
PRESS

ANOKA, MINNESOTA 2021

What Is Process Thought? Seven Answers to Seven Questions
© 2021 Process Century Press

Process Century Press
RiverHouse LLC
802 River Lane
Anoka, MN 55303

Process Century Press books are published in association with the International Process Network.

Cover: Susanna Mennicke

First presented at the Summer Academy on Process Thought in Guilin, China. Originally published by P&F Press in 2008, second printing 2010.

VOLUME VIII
THEOLOGICAL EXPLORATIONS SERIES
JEANYNE B. SLETTOM, GENERAL EDITOR

ISBN 978-1-940447-50-6
Printed in the United States of America

This series aims to explore the implications of Whiteheadian philosophy and theology for religious belief and practice. It also proposes that process religious thinkers, working from within many different traditions—Buddhist, Confucian, Christian, Hindu, Indigenous, Jewish, Muslim, and others—have unique insights pertinent to the critical issues of our day.

In 1976, we published a book, *Process Theology: An Introductory Exposition,* in which we aimed to "show the creative potentiality of a process perspective in theology." In addition to its explanation of process concepts and their application to Christian doctrine, the book noted the contribution of Whiteheadian thought toward "intercultural and interreligious understanding" and took an early stance on the ecological threat, claiming that process theology was prepared to "make a distinctive contribution" to this challenge.

Since the publication of that book, we have seen many others explore these and other themes in articles, books, and conferences. At the same time, the threat to planetary health and the need for "intercultural and interreligious understanding" has only accelerated. This series is an effort to support theologians and religious philosophers in their ongoing exposition of possible Whiteheadian solutions.

John B. Cobb, Jr.
David Ray Griffin

OTHER BOOKS IN THIS SERIES

God of Empowering Love, David P. Polk
God Exists but Gawd Does Not, David Ray Griffin
Counter-Imperial Churching for a Planetary Gospel, Timothy Murphy
Process Theology, David Ray Griffin
The Christian Gospel for Americans, David Ray Griffin
Salvation, John B. Cobb, Jr.
Reinhold Niebuhr & the Questions of Global Democracy, David Ray
    Griffin

Table of Contents

One: What is Process Thought?   1

Two: Who Is Alfred North Whitehead and
Why Are People Drawn to His Ideas?   23

Three: What Kinds of Process Thought Exist Today?   29

Four: What Are Key Ideas in Process Thought?   33

Five: What Fallacies Do Process Thinkers Try to Avoid?   37

Six: Why Do Some People Speak of Process Thought
as "Constructive Postmodernism"?   49

Seven: How Can Process Thought Be Practiced?   53

Appendices

A: The Rational Life in Whiteheadian Perspective   67

B: Culture—Propositions—Education   73

C: The Many Become One and Are Increased by One   83

D: The Principle of Universal Relativity   87

E: Beauty and the Beautiful   89

F: Practical Guidelines for Decision-Making
        (The Earth Charter)   93

Epilogue: What Is Process Theology?   95

Notes   119

What is
Process Thought?

PROCESS THOUGHT is a cultural and intellectual movement devoted to bridge-building. It builds bridges between East and West, North and South, science and spirituality, ecology and economics, education and creativity, facts and values, humanity and nature, and tradition and modernity.[1] Many of the planks of these bridges consist of ideas and practices that are drawn from the philosophy of the late philosopher and mathematician Alfred North Whitehead.[2] Thus some people speak of process thought as Whiteheadian thought.

The phrase "Whiteheadian thought" is problematic for two reasons. First, some of the fundamental ideas in process thought come from other philosophers in the early process tradition who were independent thinkers in their own right: Charles Hartshorne, Henry Nelson Weiman, Bernard Meland, and John Cobb, for

I

example. Second, many planks come from process thinkers in diverse cultures who synthesize Whiteheadian ideas with ideas from their own cultural traditions: East Asian, South Asian, African, Middle Eastern, and Chinese Marxist, for example. Process thought is an ongoing tradition that creatively synthesizes ideas from Whitehead with ideas from other sources, creating something new in each generation. Process thought is itself in process.

One way to think of process thought, then, is to envision it on the analogy of an unfinished novel in the act of being created. The first and foundational chapters of the process novel were written by Whitehead. Successive chapters were then created by Western thinkers, such as those named above, whose frames of reference lay in Western philosophy, art, science, and religion.[3] But for some years now, new chapters have been created and are being created by people in different parts of the world, whose frames of reference are not Western. In effect, they are developing *post-Western forms of process thought*. They typically employ what might be called a two-way hermeneutic. They use their own cultural resources to amplify, revise, and deepen Whitehead's ideas, and they use Whitehead's thought to interpret their traditions. This is why, today, process thinkers speak of the *international* process network.[4] Process thought began as a Western novel but its leading edge lies in its post-Western chapters.

Participants in the international process community do not seek completion of the novel. There is not a single end toward which all process thinkers aim, after which the novel would have reached its conclusion. Members of the international process community see process thought as offering ideas that can be utilized in a continuous way, into any foreseeable future, and that do not need to be called "process thought" in order to be helpful. Ultimately, process thinkers are more interested in the ideas themselves than in those ideas being recognized as "process thought."

Some process thinkers have written books articulating core ideas in the process tradition while rarely mentioning Whitehead. An example would be John Cobb's book, co-authored with Herman Daly, on economics: *For the Common Good: Redirecting the Economy Toward Community, the Environment, and a Sustainable Future.* The book is one of the most important process books of the twentieth century because it builds a bridge between economics and ecology. It addresses and then responds to the question: *What would economic theories, policies, and institutions look like if they took as their aim the promotion of human community in an ecologically responsible context, rather than ever-increasing growth?* Cobb and Daly provide answers to this question at the level of ideas, offering a philosophical anthropology for economics and also recommending policies regarding energy, taxation, and university reform. Their book is a major work in the ongoing process tradition, and yet it mentions Whitehead very little. Whitehead is in the background, not the foreground; it is the ideas that count.

What, then, are these ideas? I will introduce many of them as we go along, and list them more formally in chapter four (What Are Key Ideas in Process Thought?). But for now let me name and unpack three of them:(1) *no one crosses the same river twice;* (2) *no person is an island;* and (3) *all living beings have value.*

NO ONE CROSSES THE SAME RIVER TWICE:
BEING IS BECOMING

Consider the first saying: *no one crosses the same river twice.* Whitehead says that the whole world is fluent like a river because the world is a process of becoming, and the actual entities in the world are processes of becoming, too. Imagine a woman standing alongside a river one morning, ready to cross it by walking over a bridge as she goes to work. Process thought will say that the river she sees in the morning is not exactly the same river that she sees in the afternoon, and that the world is very much like the river. Just as the river is flowing, so the world is flowing: a network of evanescent events. Every day, even every moment, is a slightly new moment.

Process thought then adds that the woman who crosses the river is changing, too. If she crosses the river once in the morning and then crosses it again in the afternoon, the one who returns is not exactly the same as the woman who crossed in the morning. Even if she feels like the same person, she carries within her a new memory, namely, that of crossing the river earlier that morning. Her life is a process of experiencing and responding to the world, and as soon as one experience occurs, it becomes part of the past, to be followed by other experiences in the stream of experiences.

Of course, if we think in small units of time, the changes may seem insignificant. A woman early in the morning and a woman in the afternoon can seem the same to her family and friends. But if we think in larger units, the changes are obvious to the woman and to others. A woman at age 58 is not exactly the same person she was at 38, and at age 18 she is very different from who she was at age 8. Indeed, when she is 58 she can feel more identified with her friends and family who are around her than with her former self, because her life has changed so much. Her being is her becoming.

From a process perspective, the process of change over time is not predetermined by the past. All things that we see around us emerge out of a past; a woman who is 58 emerges out of experiences that she had when she was younger. But all things are also moving into a future that is open and filled with possibilities that are not yet actualized. Thus, at any given moment, human beings are like travelers on a path that has been partly paved by the past, but that remains incomplete. Their footsteps help create the path.

Moreover, even things that seem solid and unchanging— mountains, for example—are historical in nature. Geologists tell us mountains are changing over time, but their change is very slow compared to human beings. Physicists tell us that atoms change over time, but their change is extremely rapid. Mountains change in geological time; humans change in human time; atoms change in atomic time. But all things change. This means that if human beings are to find fulfillment in life, they must learn to accept the inevitability of change, learn to adapt to change, and be open to new possibilities that are not always implicit in the past. This is the first key idea: reality is process.

NO PERSON IS AN ISLAND: ALL THINGS ARE INTERCONNECTED

Now consider the second saying: No person is an island.[5] Process thought agrees with this saying, too. With geologists, process thought recognizes that real islands depend on the rivers and oceans within which they exist, and also on the geological formations that give rise to them. The islands may seem self-contained, but they can be inhabited by all kinds of creatures that were not there in earlier times, and they can disappear with the flash of a tidal wave or flood.

Process thought then adds that all living beings are in the same situation. Of course, some people may seem self-contained, because they seem unaffected by the world around them. They may lack sensitivity and care for others. But even if they are insensitive and uncaring, their very lives depend on others, both human and nonhuman. They depend on friends and family, teachers and coworkers, food and water, air and trees. Moreover, these others are part of their very identities. Even if a man tries to become like an island, shutting himself off from others, he carries within him memories of teachers and friends who have helped him over the years, and he carries within him memories of people with whom he has had problems. These other people are outside of him in some way, but also inside him as well. From a process perspective, the old idea that two things cannot be in the same place at the same time is *not* true. One human being can contain the presence of others within her own mind and body, even if those others are hundreds of miles away.

Process thought says that this is true of the whole of reality. Every entity in the universe is present in every other entity, which means that some aspect of the universe is present in each animal, each plant, each hill, each river, and each human face. When we look at a mountain, we see the history of the universe as ingredient in that mountain. When we look into the face of another, we see the universe as present in that face.

SEEING HEAVEN IN A WILDFLOWER:
ALL LIVING BEINGS HAVE VALUE

Given that "no one crosses the same river twice" and that "no man is an island," a question arises: What is the best way to live in the world? Of course, there are many possible ways of living. People may live by trying to avoid change, for example, or by trying to shut themselves off from others. Even cultures, religions, and nations can try to live this way. Process thinkers suggest, though, that these stagnant and self-enclosed ways are inconsistent with the nature of things. They say that the best way to live—the way that is in harmony with the nature of reality—is to be open to change, to be sensitive to the interconnectedness of all things, and thus to live in harmony with the deeper rhythms of the universe as a whole. To be authentically human, then, is to cooperate with these rhythms. It is to live in creative harmony with other people and the natural world in our local settings: our homes, schools, neighborhoods, workplaces, villages, and cities.

A life of creative harmony has a deeply ecological side. An ecological approach involves living with respect and care not only for human beings but also for the entire community of life. This has many practical implications. They include adopting economic policies that foster environmental protection and, at an individual level, living frugally in daily life, avoiding waste of food, water, and energy. But living with respect also involves seeing or perceiving the world in an ecologically sensitive way. From a process perspective, an ecological way of seeing can be informed by the natural sciences, but it also needs to be informed by a certain kind of aesthetic awareness or ecological wisdom.

Part of this ecological wisdom lies in seeing how individual organisms depend on other organisms for their existence. Wild-flowers, for example, depend on the sun and soil, water and clouds for their existence. They cannot exist without supportive communities. Ecological awareness involves *seeing the wildflower in its larger context*.

However, another part of this wisdom lies in seeing how larger wholes are contained in each individual entity. We might call this side of ecological awareness *seeing heaven in the wildflower*. This kind of seeing is sometimes forgotten in environmental circles. When it is forgotten environmentally, responsible people lapse into what we might call *the fallacy of neglected particularity*. This fallacy lies in forgetting the value of individual entities through excessive attention to the wholes of which they are a part. It is as if environmentalists walk into a forest and become so amazed by the splendor of the whole that they lose their capacity to pay attention to particular trees or wildflowers. They see how each part contributes to the whole, but not how the whole is contained in each part. They cannot see heaven in the wildflower.

A distinctive feature of a process approach to ecological aware-ness is that it emphasizes both modes of consciousness. It encourages people to see all living beings, humans included, as having their existence in the larger context of other living beings and the wider world. And it encourages people to see the uniqueness of each particular living being on its own terms and for its own sake. Process thought encourages us to see heaven in a wildflower and also in each human face.

One way that process thought encourages this is by talking about three kinds of value that a living being has. It has value for itself; it has value for others; and it has value for the whole. The first kind of value is called *intrinsic value* and the second two are forms of *instrumental value*. Process thought encourages us to live with respect for the intrinsic value of each living being and to make ethical decisions that take into account both forms of value. When we live in this way, we embody creative harmony.

Creative harmony is different from stagnant harmony. Stagnant harmony is achieved by trying to shut out change and remain immobile. It is the harmony of a rock as it exists alongside a road. Creative harmony is achieved by learning to adjust to new situations as they emerge in life. It is the harmony of a musician who is collaborating with other musicians to create a symphony. The *Analects* depict Confucius as developing skills in listening as he grew to become a sage: "At sixty my ears were attuned." Creative harmony lies in having ears of attunement: that is, in listening and responding to what is happening in the world.

PATTERNS OF CREATIVITY

From a process perspective, the way of creative harmony involves compassion for others. We walk in creative harmony by caring for ourselves, by contributing to the lives of others, and by appreciating the ways that others add beauty to our own lives. The others for whom we care, and who add beauty to our lives, include friends and family, neighbors and strangers. In the life of creative harmony, there can be expanding circles of sympathy. The others deserving our respect include the hills and rivers, trees and stars. We live within a universe of ten thousand things and not all of them are human. Every one of these many things, and all of them together, manifest a Creativity—an aliveness—that is not reducible to any of them, but that is expressed in their spontaneity and connections. We are never outside this larger whole; we are always already within it. Our task is to dwell creatively and harmoniously in the relationships.

These relationships are always changing. A relationship within a family can change, and so can a relationship in the workplace, the community, or among the nations. Thus the way of creative harmony is an ongoing reciprocity, give-and-take. It is open to new possibilities and to the call of each moment. No two situations are exactly alike, and creative harmony pays attention to the particularity of each situation. Of course, there are patterns within the changing world, and we can be sensitive to these patterns and learn from them: night and day, light and dark, old and new. Customs within given cultures—of greeting and speaking, marrying and mourning, eating and playing—are expressions of such patterns and so, in a very different way, are the laws of nature. These laws are habits of interaction among material entities that endure over time, and customs are habits of interaction among human beings that endure over time. But the patterns are themselves patterns of change.[6] What is new becomes old, and what is old can become new. The way of creative harmony lies in being sensitive to patterns in change and to the contexts in which those patterns are manifest.

The way of creative harmony is not limited to one culture, one philosophy, or one social setting. There are Chinese ways and American ways; secular ways and religious ways; rural ways and urban ways. Always the way is compassionate. It has a sense for the feelings of others and seeks their well-being. It knows that human beings share moods and feelings, not just words and ideas. It knows the truth of intersubjectivity.[7] And always there is a concern for common good. Those who walk in the way of creative harmony seek to build communities that are socially just, ecologically sustainable, and spiritually satisfying, with no one left behind. They know that the suffering of one person belongs to all people.

It is with ideas such as those identified above, then, that process thinkers seek to help the world. As noted, one way they do this is by bridge building. Perhaps it can further a provisional understanding of process thought if I offer three examples. Consider first a bridge between *education and cosmology*.[8]

Example 1: Education and Cosmology

One of the key ideas of process thought is that education can and should do two things at once. It should (1) enable a student to live responsibly and compassionately in society, respecting other people and the natural world, and also (2) inspire a student's curiosity about the world and help a student develop his or her creative potential. In short, education should give a student a sense of security and adventure—of roots and wings—with neither one to the exclusion of the other.

This idea has obvious relevance to attempts at educational reform today. The purpose of these reforms is to develop ways in which students can develop their creative potentials (the wing side) and develop a sense of civic responsibility and concern for others (the root side). As educators work on these reforms, their efforts can be frustrated by assumptions concerning *learning* that permeate society. Contrary to the spirit of the reforms, ordinary citizens, including parents and administrators, can assume that genuine learning is *passive learning*. By passive learning I mean learning amid which students acquire facts—isolated bits of information— from teachers without adding anything of their own to those facts. Given a philosophy of passive learning, a student's performance is appropriately measured in terms of whether he or she can reproduce those facts on objective exams. There is no need for reform. Behind this view of learning is a vision of human beings as passive receptacles for facts and of the universe itself as a vast collection of isolated facts. The student is not very creative, and neither is the universe.

Process thinkers propose that this mechanistic view of the universe is scientifically outdated. They believe that the frontiers of science point toward a more organic universe in which the genuine building blocks of the universe are events, each of which is a creative synthesis of inherited influences, into something slightly new. Their argument is that even pulsations of energy within the depths of atoms are acts of synthesis. Process thinkers suggest further that the universe as a whole is itself an ongoing process of change which is, in Whitehead's words, "creative advance into novelty" (PR 349). At any given moment of time, the universe is shaped by what it has been in the past, but also drawn toward what it can be in the , uture. Thus each building block in the universe has roots and wings, and so does the universe as a whole.

This vision of a creative universe offers cosmological support for the kinds of educational reforms sought by educators throughout the world. Inspired by a process understanding of the universe, educators can affirm a harmony between the dynamics of the universe and the dynamics of the human mind. Educators can argue that human curiosity—openness to novelty—is not simply a means to the end of human happiness; it is also a human way of being attuned to the deeper promptings of the universe. And they can argue that the human need to dwell compassionately in community with others is likewise a way of being attuned to those promptings. The aims of education and the aims of the universe coalesce.

Example 2: Science and Spirituality

Or consider a Whiteheadian bridge between science and spirituality. A key idea in the process tradition is that science does indeed reveal factual information about the universe. In particular, science illuminates causal connections that can be verified by experimentation and articulated through mathematical analysis. Process thinkers approach science as critical realists. They believe that the methods of science are akin to a flashlight that illuminates certain aspects of the natural world, including human life, that might not otherwise be apparent.

Another key idea in the process tradition is that aesthetic awareness also tells us something about the natural world. For Whitehead, we learn something about nature by walking through a forest and sensing the beauty of the flowers, trees, and waterways. In the West, the nature poetry of William Wordsworth conveys this sense that the natural world, when apprehended with deep sensitivity, reveals a beauty and presence beyond words. Whitehead believes that aesthetic apprehension is complementary to scientific apprehension, helping complete it. Deeply felt intuitions, too, are like flashlights that illumine something about nature.

Whitehead recognizes multiple ways of knowing and offers a worldview in which they can be jointly affirmed and harmonized. For example, sometimes—when science is at its best—a scientific understanding of nature can increase our sense of its beauty because we find ourselves amazed by its structure. If spirituality includes an appreciation of nature's beauty, then there is a link between science and spirituality. The aims of science and the aims of spirituality are not discordant. They are harmonized.

Of course some people use the word "spirituality" to name something more than a sense of appreciation for nature's beauty. Some in China will use it to refer to feelings and acts of kindness or compassion, for example. And some in the West will use it to refer to faith or trust in a higher power or deeper ground to existence. In the West, this higher power or deeper ground is typically named God. In our time, the word "spirituality" can have many different meanings, all of which are appropriate in different contexts.

Whitehead's philosophy shows how other kinds of spirituality are also consonant with modern science. For example, with help from Whitehead and evolutionary biology, we see how human kindness is an amplification of, not an exception to, impulses toward cooperation and empathy that are found in other animals; and at the same time we see how the evolution of kindness, as a form of adaptation, can be partly inspired by a divine reality at the heart of the universe. Much work has been done on these matters by a process thinker whom some consider the "dean" of contemporary dialogues between religion and science: Ian Barbour. His book *God, Humanity, and Human Nature* offers clear explanations of many connections between science and spirituality.

Example 3: Economic Development and Environmental Protection

Finally, let us consider how process thinkers link economics and environmental protection. In modern times, a great deal of emphasis is placed on economic development. China is a remarkable example of such development amid which millions of people have been lifted from poverty. Process thinkers celebrate this. One of the major ideas in process thought is that every human being is a subject of his or her life and deserves respect and care. Humans are ends in themselves and not simply means to other ends. No human being deserves to live in poverty.

Another idea in process thought is that all things are interconnected, and thus that human beings are part of the larger whole of nature. This means that economic development cannot be sharply separated from respecting and protecting nature. There can and must be a bridge between economic development and environmental protection, such that the two go hand in hand.

Moreover, the process perspective points beyond an ethic of environmental protection toward what might be called an ethic of deep ecology—an ethic that places humans within nature as a larger whole, and that is grounded in a sense of respect for the whole.

This is the direction in which Whitehead's philosophy points. An ethic of deep ecology does not stop with nature as something to protect; it moves forward into the image of nature as a womb-like whole in which humans are small but included. From a Whiteheadian perspective, people can and should aim at developing cities and villages that are grounded in a sense of deep ecology; that is, a spiritual sense of a greater whole. We might call them eco-villages and eco-cities.

Thus we have three bridges that are important to process thinkers: education and cosmology, science and spirituality, and economics and ecology. There are many others, and all are important to people in the international process network.

PROCESS THINKERS

Today, the members of this international network come from different walks of life. Some are philosophers in a formal or professional sense. By this I mean that they teach in departments of philosophy in different parts of the world, and that they are trained in the history of philosophy. Typically, they are not content simply to teach about the history of philosophy; they seek to do some constructing of their own. They think of themselves as constructive philosophers. However, many other participants in the process movement are not professional philosophers. They teach in disciplines such as biology, physics, education, business, literature, and the arts. They use Whitehead's thought to interpret aspects of their own traditions, developing "Whiteheadian" approaches to their subjects. Moreover, many others are ordinary citizens at work in the world as entrepreneurs, government workers, poets, accountants, priests, and farmers. They apply principles of process thought to their activities and undertakings in the real world.

In using the phrase "process thinkers" rather than process philosophers, I am saying that not all are philosophers in the formal or academic sense. They are not trained in the history of philosophy nor do they teach in philosophy departments. But all are philosophers in the general sense of being interested in living from wisdom. If philosophy means loving wisdom, all process thinkers are philosophers. Given the many different kinds of people who embrace process points of view, it might be best to call process thought a wisdom tradition.

A wisdom tradition includes all aspects of a person's life, the cultural side as well as the intellectual side. Culture includes feeling and perception and action. In process thought, thinking and feeling are understood to be closely connected. Even thinking is a form of feeling. Wisdom is not simply a matter of having good ideas. Wisdom is also a matter of seeing and perceiving the world in a sensitive way and of interacting with others in creative and compassionate ways. A person can have good ideas but not be very wise. Process thought is interested in promoting good ideas, but it is even more interested in fostering wisdom.

In process thought, bridge-building is itself a form of wisdom. Because everything is connected to everything else, it is "wise" to unveil connections and seek to live in light of those connections. For most process thinkers, the purpose of building the bridges is not simply to satisfy the intellectual curiosity of scholars in the university, or to satisfy the more personal questions of citizens in ordinary life, or to advance knowledge within the modern university. It is to offer ideas that can help bring about communities throughout the world that are *creative, compassionate, equitable, participatory, ecologically wise, scientifically informed, and spiritually satisfying, with no one left behind.* We can call them "sustainable" communities. They are sustainable in the sense that they provide sustenance for human life and also in the sense that they can be sustained into the foreseeable future, given the limits of the Earth to absorb pollution and renew resources. The guiding ideal of such communities will be *respect and care for the community of life.* This is the guiding ideal of the process tradition.[9]

Process thinkers celebrate the fact that seeds of these kinds of sustainable community already exist in different parts of the world, and that many people are working to build these communities without any knowledge of, or interest in, process thought. Some are young and some are old; some are Buddhist and some are Christian; some are Marxist and some are Republican. Indeed, many process thinkers fall into these categories. Process thought is not a sect that excludes other identities. It is an intellectual and cultural movement that can accommodate and include many different points of view, both nonreligious and religious. Thus process thinkers seek to work in collaboration with people from all walks of life, process-oriented or otherwise, who are also interested in sustainable community: government officials, artists, businessmen, school teachers, scientists, clerks, and farmers.

In the process tradition, collaboration is reciprocal practice. On the one hand, process thinkers believe that ideas in process thought can truly help people build sustainable communities. On the other hand, they recognize that other people have good ideas, too. Part of the process tradition is democratic in spirit. It lies in the belief that there is much wisdom in the minds and hearts of people from all walks of life, and that process thought does not itself have all the answers.

This has implications for a process approach to ethics. For process thinkers, it is not enough to talk to others and share one's ideas. And it is not enough simply to act on one's ideas. It is also important to *listen* to others in a spirit of respect and have the humility to learn from them. This listening involves a willingness to be changed. Thus process thinkers are committed to what one American philosopher, John Churchill, calls the deliberative life. Insights emerge from mutual deliberation that could not emerge otherwise, and in the act of deliberation it is fine—even good—if there are disagreements. In process thought, the act of listening to others and learning from them, and also sharing with others and having them learn from you, is sometimes called *creative transformation*. Creative transformation is not simply an active or willful activity. It involves allowing one's own mental and spiritual horizons to widen in the process of receiving influences from others.

Of course, people can resist creative transformation. We do it all the time. We close ourselves off from opportunities to learn from others and be in dialogue with them. We want to arrive at a place in life where there will be no more changes. But from a process perspective this resistance is doomed to fail because change is inescapable. In process thought, the actual world *is* a process.

THE WORD "PROCESS"

The word *process* does not necessarily mean progress. Things can get worse as well as better. But the word process does mean *change*. For process thinkers, even when things seem to stay the same, there is a passage of time and thus change. Things are not separate from the passage of time; the passage of time is part of the very being of entities. In the twentieth century, in the West, Martin Heidegger wrote a famous book called *Being and Time* in which he proposed that human life is essentially temporal. There cannot be human being without temporality, a sense of past and future. Process thinkers agree and suggest that the whole of reality is temporal. Thus process thinkers see the universe on the analogy of verbs rather than nouns. Molecules, animals, plants, hills, rivers, trees, stars, people, cultures, religions, and nations—all are acts of becoming that change, even if only slightly, through their interactions with others. To be is to inherit from a past and be drawn toward a future. To be is to become.

Of course, this is not the whole story. Process thinkers say there are patterns that endure over time, giving the world structure and the appearance of constancy amidst change. Whitehead speaks of these patterns as pure potentialities that may be embodied in the world over and over again. As embodied in the actual world, we see these patterns all the time. We enter a building one day and then again on the following; it seems to be the same building from one day to the next. The bricks are in the same place; the rooms are arranged in the same way; the patterns are roughly the same. But process thinkers believe that, deep down, the energetic dynamics of the atoms and molecules composing the bricks and rooms are in process, as are the people who enter the buildings and then leave them. The person who enters the building tomorrow will be slightly changed by the experiences she undergoes today. In every moment of experience things are slightly new, both in people and in buildings.

This holds true for historical traditions, as well. Hegel pointed out that traditions can be understood not simply as what they have been in the past, but also what they are becoming and what they can be in the future. A tradition can unfold over time and even embody new possibilities that were not embodied in its past, but which add to it. This is why process thought is best called a *movement* rather than a *system* or even a *worldview*. Process thinkers are inclined to see all traditions as movements: religious traditions, scientific traditions, cultural traditions. They do not have timeless essences; they are historical through and through. Traditions are *movements*. Movements flow and change over time, building upon what has happened in the past but adding new things in the future. There is a proverb which says that, as people travel through life, their footsteps help create the path. As process thinkers develop their ideas, their thinking creates process thought.

Process thinkers believe that one important way of finding wisdom in life is by learning from the historical traditions in which one is nested. In process thought, these historical traditions are not simply cultural treasures, they are also *islands of possibility*. They contain within them rich possibilities for the future, if critically appropriated and creatively transformed. Sometimes we can look to the past to find the future.

THE FUTURE IN PROCESS THOUGHT

Of course, this raises the question: What is the future? In process thought, the future does not exist as something actual. It only exists in the form of myriad potentialities that may or may not be "actualized" in the present. Many process thinkers believe in God, but they do not think that God knows the future in advance. God is in process along with the universe. Still, humans do indeed look to the future in their daily lives. Human life is forward-looking as well as past-respecting. Humans are guided by anticipation as well as memory. When we anticipate the future, what is the object we are anticipating?

The answer must be *possibilities*. In process thought the possibilities of the future can be felt through various emotions: dread, fear, anxiety, hope, excitement, and happy expectation. Whitehead calls these emotions subjective forms. Many humans fear the future, but process thinkers are especially interested in the more promising ways of experiencing it. The very hope for sustainable communities, or for educational reform, or for a socialist society, or for peace on Earth presupposes that the future can be felt through hope rather than dread. We might naturally ask: When people feel the presence of the future in this more promising way, what exactly are they feeling? The answer process thinkers give is: *novel possibilities*. A novel possibility is a possibility that feels new, relative to the situation at hand.

The evolution of process thought is itself an example of openness to novel possibilities. Recall the analogy at the outset of this essay, in which I compared process thought to the ongoing composition of a novel. Since the early periods of the process movement, many new chapters have been created, and sometimes they take the "plot" of process thought in directions that Whitehead would appreciate but did not imagine. For example, Whitehead did not systematically address environmental problems, and yet many use his ideas to develop philosophies of environmental ethics. Whitehead did not develop a theology for Christians or a philosophy for Buddhists, yet both have used his thought for these purposes, using his thought to develop contemporary forms of religious thought that are complementary to the natural sciences. Whitehead did not develop a systematic interpretation of evolutionary biology or quantum theory, but Whitehead's philosophy has been used by biologists and physicists to develop such interpretations. In undertaking these actions, scholars are adding new chapters to the ongoing tradition of process thought.

UNIVERSAL PROCESS THOUGHT

Many people believe Whitehead's philosophy is closer to Chinese ways of thinking than it is to Western ways. Whitehead himself believed that his way of thinking resembles Asian more than Western ways in some of its fundamental emphases. In fact, some process thinkers distinguish between Whiteheadian process thought and universal process thought. Universal process thought consists of ideas important to the Whiteheadian tradition that are found in other cultures and perhaps better expressed in those cultures. Here are some very general ideas that are important to Whiteheadians and which, from a Whiteheadian point of view, would be part of the more universal tradition:

- Everything is in process; reality is flowing; nothing ever stays the same.

- All things are interconnected; no human is an island; things are present in one another even as they have their autonomy.

- The whole of nature has value; all living beings deserve respect; human beings are not the sole repository of value.

- Human beings find happiness in sharing experiences with

others; there are no isolated egos; all selves are selves-in-relation; humans become whole through reciprocity.

- The essence of the universe is a continuous creativity of which all things are expressions; there is creativity in plants and animals, hills and rivers, trees and stars.

- All beings seek harmony as their guiding ideal; harmony includes differences; the whole of the universe is a harmony of harmonies.

- Thinking and emotion cannot be sharply separated; mind and body are not two; even thinking is a form of feeling; aesthetic wisdom and rational inquiry are complementary.

- Every moment of human experience begins, not with projecting things onto the world or even acting in the world, but with feeling the presence of the world and being affected by it.

Such ideas are very important to Whiteheadian thinkers, but they are not unique to Whitehead. Students of Chinese culture know that such ideas have existed in China since the dawn of Chinese civilization. Some people say—only half in jest—that Whitehead's thought is a Western way of catching up with Chinese ways of thinking and adding science to the mix.

Who Is
Alfred North Whitehead?

And Why Are People
Drawn to His Ideas?

WHITEHEAD (1861–1947) WAS A MATHEMATICIAN and a philosopher who was born in England and moved, late in his life, to the United States, where he taught at Harvard. Whitehead's interests were wide-ranging. His corpus of work is sometimes divided into three periods. The first period corresponds with his time at Cambridge, from 1884 to 1910. This is the period in which he worked with Bertrand Russell on *Principia Mathematica*. The second corresponds with his time in London from 1910 to 1924. During these years, Whitehead focused on the philosophy of science and the philosophy of education. The third period corresponds with his time at Harvard, from 1924 onward. It was during this time that he worked on more general issues in philosophy, including the development of a comprehensive metaphysical system that has come to be known as process philosophy.

The books written by Whitehead that have most influenced the process movement are: *Science and the Modern World* (1925); *Religion in the Making* (1926); *Symbolism, Its Meaning and Effect,* (1927); *The Aims of Education and Other Essays* (1929); *The Function of Reason* (1929); *Process and Reality* (1929); *Adventures of Ideas* (1933); *Nature and Life* (1934); and *Modes of Thought* (1938). His cosmology, or metaphysical perspective, is articulated most systematically in *Process and Reality,* which is also one of the most difficult books to read in the English language.

Whitehead's mature philosophy was influenced by two kinds of Western sources: scientific and humanistic. On the one hand, he was deeply influenced by modern science, especially early quantum theory, evolutionary biology, and relativity theory. His earliest work was in mathematics and the philosophy of science. On the other hand, he was also influenced by numerous traditions in Western intellectual and aesthetic history: the philosophy of Plato, the poetry of William Wordsworth, the empiricism of the John Locke and David Hume, the pragmatism of William James, and the spirituality of Christianity.

A unique feature of Whitehead's thought is that he believed that each of these sources yields wisdom concerning the universe and human life within it. Thus he was a deeply interdisciplinary thinker. In his most systematic work, *Process and Reality,* he integrated insights from numerous traditions—scientific, artistic, ethical, and religious—into a single, comprehensive worldview. This is part of what draws many thinkers to Whitehead's perspective. It helps overcome intellectual fragmentation by offering a "big picture" of the world and human life. Philosophers and others are often eager to place Whitehead in a particular lineage of Western philosophy. Was he a rationalist or an empiricist? Was he a pragmatist or an idealist? Was he in the Continental tradition or the Anglo-American tradition?

Those who know his thought well often find it very difficult to place him, because the influences that shaped his life and thought were so varied. Sometimes he is placed in the pragmatist tradition of American philosophy, sometimes in the process-oriented traditions of German Idealism, sometimes in the phenomenological traditions of Heidegger and Husserl, and sometimes in the more pluralistically oriented traditions of postmodernism. He himself felt sympathies for Plato, and is noted as saying that Western philosophy is but a series of footnotes to Plato. Perhaps the difficulty lies in the fact that much of his training was in mathematics and science, and he did not feel a need to link himself more exclusively with a distinct philosophical tradition. Nevertheless, PhD dissertations have been written that compare his thinking with many Western thinkers: Plato, Aristotle, Descartes, Kant, Nietzsche, and many others.

In terms of the question of rationalism or empiricism, Whitehead thought of himself as being in *both* traditions. He took the realm of ideas very seriously, and believed that ideas have a kind of reality (as possibilities) that cannot be reduced to materiality or the actual world, and yet Whitehead also believed that they lack capacities for power and decision until acted upon (and actualized) by earthly events. He believed that a philosophy should be evaluated, not only in terms of the coherence of its ideas, but also (and very importantly) in terms of its adequacy to experience. Some people understand Whitehead's philosophy as a philosophy of experience and note further that, for him, experience includes all kinds of experience beside sense-perception: experience asleep and experience awake, experience anxious and experience carefree, experience conscious and experience subconscious, experience drunk and experience sober (AI 226). He wanted to develop a philosophy that was adequate to the whole range of human experience and that could help humans interpret the wider world. (For further information on Whitehead's method, see Appendix A).

Whitehead's emphasis on experience also puts him in tension with language philosophers and the analytic tradition. He believed

that propositions were not reducible to their linguistic expressions
and could be expressed in many different languages, and he believed
that there are many forms of wisdom that are not easily verbalized.
Whitehead developed a philosophy of language, but he also thinks
that experience is not reducible to language and that there is much
to talk about in philosophy besides language.

Whitehead hoped that his own "big picture" would be evaluated,
critiqued, revised, and, if needed, rejected. He did not think it was
the final answer to all important questions, and he was opposed
to all forms of overly dogmatic or arrogant thinking. At the end
of the preface to *Process and Reality,* he writes:

> There remains the final reflection, how shallow, puny and
> imperfect are efforts to sound the depths in the nature
> of things. In philosophical discussion the merest hint
> of dogmatic certainty as to finality of statement is an
> exhibition of folly. (PR xiv)

It is in this spirit, then, that Whitehead offers his big picture or, to
use a more philosophical term, his metaphysical perspective. He
knew that his own point of view would be transformed over time.

Why, then, are people drawn to Whitehead and his ideas? In
addition to offering a big picture, here are some other reasons.

The big questions. Many people turn to Whitehead because
they want to help people address the big questions in life such as
"What is truly important in life?" and "What does it mean to be
human?" and "How are human beings situated within the larger
context of the natural world?" and "What is the nature of nature?"
The process tradition offers quite specific and carefully thought out
responses to these kinds of questions, drawing upon insights from
scientific experience, moral experience, and aesthetic experience. It
offers a rationally plausible worldview for modern times.

The advance of scholarship. Some people turn to Whitehead
because they believe aspects of process thought can advance

distinctive lines of inquiry within academic life itself, including inquiries in the arts and sciences. For example, process thinkers with scientific interests use ideas in Whitehead's thought to help interpret evolutionary biology, quantum theory, chaos theory, and various aspects of relativity theory. Process thinkers with interests in the humanities use process thought to interpret film, literature, music, and the performing arts.

Transdisciplinarity. Some turn to Whitehead because they believe that his thought can help scholars in the modern university overcome the disciplinary fragmentation that too often prevents them from communicating with one another and addressing the more pressing needs of the world. Process thinkers believe there is value in disciplinary specialization, but this value also has its limitations. Process thought is indeed a transdisciplinary approach to modern life, helping people address problems that can only be addressed in a transdisciplinary way. An example would be ecological problems. These problems are not the specialized province of scientists or political theorists or economics or cultural theorists; they require more holistic responses amid which scholars can bring their specialized expertise, but also "think outside the box" of overly specialized approaches.

Guidance for educational and public policy. Some find Whitehead's thought helpful in guiding organizations—governments, schools, and businesses, for example—as they develop laws, curricula, and business practices. An example would be the work of process thinkers designing goals for education (Robert Regnier, Bob Mesle, Marcus Ford, and Sandra Lubarsky) and recommending policies for economic activity (John Cobb, Herman Daly).

Cultural transformation. Some process thinkers—Zhihe Wang, for example—find Whitehead's thought important because it points towards forms of cultural transformation that offer a creative and value-centered alternative to the dilemmas of "rootless consumerism" and "stagnant traditionalism" that often permeate modern societies. For further information on a Whiteheadian approach to culture, see Appendix B.

These are not the only reasons that process thinkers are drawn to Whitehead's point of view and, clearly, many of these reasons are connected.

What Kinds of Process Thought Exist Today?

IT IS IN LIGHT of some of the reasons named above that process thinkers have developed myriad forms of process thought. Here is a small list of the kinds available:

Whiteheadian metaphysics offers an organic worldview that integrates insights from science, aesthetics, spirituality, and ethics into a single, integrative way of looking at the world. This worldview helps show how the many dimensions of the world are part of a single and dynamic whole. It overcomes many dualisms that have been part of Western philosophy, especially the dualisms between fact and value, mind and body, humanity and nature, thinking and feeling.

Whiteheadian philosophies of science apply aspects of Whitehead's thought to quantum theory, evolutionary biology, relativity theory, and other more specialized topics within science, and also to general philosophical questions concerning the nature of science. Typically, they embrace an approach to science that can be called critical realism. This approach avoids the idea that science merely projects ideas onto the world, and the idea that scientific ideas are mere instruments for practical purposes. But it also avoids the idea that science is a completely objective rendition of the world, devoid of any interpretive nature. It says that science illuminates aspects of the natural world and that there is an objective world to be understood, but also that human approaches to the natural world—including scientific approaches—are inevitably interpretive and theory-laden. Thus there is no perfectly objective approach to nature, but also no simply private approach. Critical realism says that human beings are part of nature; that their interactions with nature are also part of nature, and that science itself is a form of interaction in which qualities of nature are revealed.

Whiteheadian social philosophies offer guidelines for building sustainable communities. Some of these social philosophies focus on economic dimensions of life, developing what might be called process approaches to economics. Others focus on questions of personal morality, law, and politics. All emphasize the importance of adding ecological considerations to images of community well-being, and all are grounded in Whiteheadian theories of value. Process social philosophies have given rise to process approaches to business ethics, urban development, rural development, and management theory.

Whiteheadian theories of value emphasize that all living beings have value in themselves, for one another, and for the larger whole. Value can refer to the intrinsic value of each living being, to the instrumental value of living beings for others and the whole. But value can also refer to ideals and goals that animate and guide human action. The idea of a sustainable community is a value of the latter sort. We might call it a social value. The value that human beings have for themselves is a value of the first sort. It is an example of intrinsic value. And the value that human beings have for others—for friends and family—would be an example of instrumental value. Whiteheadian theories of value emphasize all of these kinds. In addition, they highlight beauty as the ultimate value to which all living beings are drawn. Beauty consists of harmony and intensity in experience. (See Appendix E.)

Whiteheadian philosophies of education offer ideas concerning pedagogy, curriculum, and the aims of education that are conducive to the emergence of such communities and that offer possibilities for educational reform. These educational philosophies are oriented, not only toward the acquisition of practical skills, but also toward encouraging creativity, originality, and a sense of service among students of all ages. Emphasis is placed on education as a lifelong process. A central idea in a process attached to value is to say that the educational process itself involves rhythms of romance, precision, and generalization. Romance refers to the excitement a person feels when first encountering a new idea and sensing its many possibilities; precision refers to the act of learning more about the idea or skill, entering into detailed study and application; and generalization involves taking the idea or skill and applying it to other subjects and areas.

Whiteheadian philosophies of culture and daily life point to ways of living in the world—available to people from many walks of life—that are harmonious, creative, and spiritually satisfying. These philosophies of culture typically emphasize harmony and creativity as guiding ideals for a meaningful way of living in the world, both of which are understood as forms of beauty.

Whiteheadian philosophies of spirituality, religion, and interreligious dialogue address religious questions. The philosophies of religion typically take a world religions approach, seeing the many world religions as containing different kinds of truth, each worth affirming. And the philosophical theologies develop particular points of view that help advance a distinctive religious perspective. Process Christian theology is an example of the latter. (See Epilogue.)

What Are Key Ideas
in Process Thought?

A T THIS POINT, many of the core ideas have already been presented. And, while process thinkers recognize that ideas can be expressed in word, many process ideas can be better expressed through the arts and certainly through actions. In any case, here is one sample of key ideas.

Process: The universe is an ongoing process of development and change, never quite the same at any two moments. Every entity in the universe is best understood as a process of becoming that emerges through its interactions with others.

Interconnectedness: The universe as a whole is a seamless web of interconnected events, none of which can be completely separated from the others. Everything is connected to everything else and contained in everything else.

Continuous creativity: The universe exhibits a continuous

creativity on the basis of which new events come into existence over time that did not exist. This continuous creativity is the ultimate reality of the universe.

The value of nature: The natural world has value in itself, and all living beings are worthy of respect and care. Rocks and trees, hills and rivers, are not simply facts in the world; they are also acts of self-realization.

Harmony: Humans find their fulfillment in living harmony with the Earth and compassionately with each other. Harmony is not sameness.

Novelty: The future does not exist prior to its emergence except as possibility. The universe is a "creative advance into novelty." Humans find their fulfillment in being open to new ideas, insights, and experiences that may have no parallel in the past.

Thinking and feeling: The human mind is not limited to reasoning but also includes feeling, intuiting, imagining. All of these activities can work together toward understanding. Even reasoning is a form of feeling; that is, feeling the presence of ideas and responding to them.

The self as person-in-community: Human beings are not skin-encapsulated egos cut off from the world by the boundaries of the skin, but persons-in-community whose interactions with others are partly definitive of their own internal existence.

Complementary thinking. The rational life consists not only of identifying facts and appealing to evidence, but taking apparently conflicting ideas and showing how they can be woven into wholes, with each side contributing to the other. In Whitehead's thought, these wholes are called contrasts.

Theory and practice: Theory affects practice and practice affects theory; a dichotomy between the two is false. What people do affects how they think and how they think affects what they do. Learning can occur from body to mind; that is, by doing things and not simply from mind to body.

The primacy of persuasion over coercion: There are two ways to practice power—coercively and persuasively—and the latter is to be preferred. Coercive power is the power of force and violence; persuasive power is the power of invitation and moral example.

The power of relationality: This is experienced when people dwell in mutually enhancing relations, such that both are empowered through their relations with one another. In international relations, this would be the kind of empowerment that occurs when governments enter into trade relations that are mutually beneficial and serve the wider society; in parenting, this would be the power that parents and children enjoy when, even amid a hierarchical relationship, there is respect on both sides, and the relationship strengthens parents and children.

The primacy of particularity: There is a difference between ideas that are abstracted from concrete events in the world and the events themselves. The fallacy of misplaced concreteness lies in confusing the abstractions with the concrete events and focusing more on the abstract than the particular.

Experience in the mode of causal efficacy: Human experience is not restricted to acting on things or actively interpreting a passive world. It begins by a conscious and unconscious receiving of events into life and being causally affected or influenced by what is received. This occurs through the mediation of the body but can also occur through a reception of the moods and feelings of other people (and animals).

Concern for the vulnerable: Humans are gathered together in a web of felt connections, such that they share in one another's sufferings and are responsible to one another. Humans can share feelings and be affected by one another's feelings in a spirit of mutual sympathy.

Education as a lifelong process: Human life is itself a journey from birth (and perhaps before) to death (and perhaps after), and the journey is itself a process of character development over time.

Formal education in the classroom is a context to facilitate the process, but the process continues throughout a lifetime.

These are not the only ideas important to process thinkers. Those who are deeply involved in the sciences would want to add ideas concerning evolution, astrophysics, chaos theory, entropy, and order. And religiously oriented process thinkers would add something about Whitehead's understanding of God. A special word about the latter is important here.

GOD IN WHITEHEAD'S THOUGHT

Whitehead did indeed develop a way of thinking about God that is attractive to many process thinkers and, for some, is at the very heart of his perspective. But his way of thinking about God is very different from traditional understandings in the West. Whitehead did not think of God as a separate being cut off from the world by the boundaries of divine transcendence; nor did he think of God as precisely identical with the universe and its creative energies. Whitehead thought of God as an expression of, not an exception to, the creativity of the universe; God functions in the universe as a counter-entropic lure, helping to bring order and novelty into the world, and also as a receptacle for all the world's happenings. For Whitehead, God is both everywhere and nowhere. God is everywhere, being equally present to all things, and nowhere, because there is an aspect of God that is simply non-spatial. He believed that God is the Harmony of Harmonies and thus the subjective unity of the universe as a whole.

Some process thinkers find Whitehead's notion of God extremely valuable; some are not as interested in it; and some explicitly reject it. For all of them, there is a spiritual side to life, but some emphasize the spirituality that resides in meaningful connections with others and with the natural world, rather than the spirituality that might lie in faith or trust in God. The former seems more Confucian in spirit; the latter more Abrahamic.

What Fallacies Do Process
Thinkers Try to Avoid?

STILL ANOTHER WAY to characterize the process tradition is to identify some fallacies which, from a Whiteheadian point of view, need to be avoided in human life. Already, I have mentioned the fallacy of misplaced concreteness. Here are some others.

- The fallacy of substance thinking
- The fallacy of subject-predicate ontology
- The fallacy of hopelessness (life without possibility)
- The fallacy of stagnant harmony
- The fallacy of misplaced creativity
- The fallacy of unbridgeable cultural gaps
- The fallacy of the perfect dictionary
- The fallacy of simple location

These are not merely logical or intellectual fallacies. They are emotional and attitudinal fallacies, and often they are embodied in people's lives quite apart from conscious choice. They are habitual modes of consciousness, promulgated by cultural factors, that can develop within an individual or a community over time. These habits of the heart and mind prevent people from becoming their better selves.

THE FALLACY OF SUBSTANCE THINKING

The fallacy of substance thinking has two aspects. The first lies in believing that the truly real entities in the universe—whatever they happen to be—are self-enclosed "substances" that could exist and be defined quite apart from their relations with other entities. Thus their relations are external to their existence, rather than internal to their existence. The second lies in thinking that the truly real entities in the universe endure unchanged over time. When these two ideas are put together, we have the image of a "substance" as something that endures unchanged over time and whose relations are external to its existence. Whitehead's entire philosophy is meant to present an alternative to this way of thinking.

Generally speaking, process philosophers propose that the being or existence of an entity—its internal essence—is a *process of becoming,* and that this process occurs *through its interactions with other entities.* Whereas non-relational visions might picture atoms, molecules, living cells, and human beings as self-contained fact, process visions picture them as creative syntheses of relations with others. Whereas static visions might picture them as having their existence apart from their interactions, process visions picture them as having their existence through their interactions. Whitehead puts it this way: "There are no self-sustained facts, floating in nonentity" and "how an entity becomes constitutes what that entity is" (PR 11, 23).

THE FALLACY OF SUBJECT-PREDICATE ONTOLOGY

This fallacy is at the heart of substance thinking. It lies in projecting the subject-predicate grammatical structure onto reality itself, and thus thinking that the truly real entities of the universe mirror this grammatical structure. In static and non-relational visions of reality a subtle but false identification is often made between the *nature of existence* and the *structure of language*. To be specific, an entity's existence is imagined on the analogy of a grammatical subject within a sentence that has a clearly defined subject and predicate. In the subject-predicate mode of grammatical expression, the subjects of our sentences often remain the same even as the predicates change. We say "The woman goes to the store" and then "The woman goes to the movie" and then "The woman is talking to the man"—and we assume that the woman remains the same even as the predicates change. From the more static perspective, the same situation applies to the world beyond language: namely, the physical or material world of hills, rivers, plants, animals, and people. It can seem as if hills and rivers and people are like subjects of sentences, and that they remain the same even as their actions in the world and relations with the world change.

Process philosophers disagree with this point of view. They say that as the predicates change, the subjects change, too. Of course, certain patterns may recur again and again. In the history of an atom or a human being, certain forms or patterns will appear and re-appear. But the entities themselves—the atom and the person— are slightly different at every moment, because the world is different at every moment, and their own existence, moment by moment, emerges through interaction with that world. To repeat Whitehead: "How an entity becomes constitutes what that entity is."

Consider the sentence "The woman is talking to the man." The subject of the sentence would be "the woman" and the predicate would be "is talking to the man." A static worldview would say that the woman's being—her internal essence—is independent of the act of talking to the man. The woman is a self-contained entity, locked inside her skin, who is witness to the act of talking but who is not really affected by the talking. A more dynamic or process-oriented worldview will say that her very existence is slightly changed by the conversation, such that the woman who leaves the conversation is not precisely the same as the woman who began it. Of course the conversation with the man may not be very important to her. It may not have changed her personality or opinions in the least. Indeed she may forget it soon afterwards and turn to other matters, almost as if it never occurred. Nevertheless, from a process perspective, it will affect her in some small way. When she departs the conversation, her life will contain a memory which, prior to the conversation, it lacked. Her being cannot be separated from her actions in the world and her interactions with others.

THE FALLACY OF HOPELESSNESS (LIFE WITHOUT POSSIBILITY)

The phrase "fallacy of hopelessness" is a phrase of my own invention, but it captures an idea essential to Whitehead; namely that in whatever situation a person might find himself or herself, there is always a possibility of a novel or creative response to the situation at hand. That novel response may simply be the lesser of evils. If a man is dying of cancer, for example, his "novel response" may simply be to face his death with courage rather than fear. If a man is in prison, his "novel response" may simply be to make the best of a bad situation.

The fallacy of hopelessness, then, is the idea that there can be no new beginnings in life, because a person's existence is entirely determined by what has happened in the past and what is happening in the present. The alternative recommended by process thinkers is to recognize two things: (1) that a human life unfolds over time, moment by moment, and that in every moment a new self emerges that did not exist beforehand; and (2) that, no matter how difficult a situation, there is always a window of possibility for creatively responding to the situation at hand and thus making something new out of the old. In the case of the man dying from cancer, the new beginning is the courage that can emerge in his life, with help from others, even as he is about to die. Novelty is possible.

Sometimes poetry better expresses this constructive point better than philosophy. In the West, there is a poem by Walt Whitman called "There was a Child Went Forth." It depicts a child who becomes what he or she experiences:

> There was a child went forth every day,
> And the first object he looked upon, that object he became
> And that object became part of him for the day or a certain
>   part of the day,
> Or for many years or stretching cycles of years.

The poem goes on to explain how the child's mother and father became part of the child, and how the child's friends and teachers became part of the child, and how the good things and bad things that happened to the child became part of him, too. Even when the child becomes an adult, the child will be "going forth every day" and being slightly changed by what he or she experiences including the surrounding sights of the city streets: "men and women crowding fast in the streets" and "the streets themselves and the façades of the houses, and goods in the windows." The poem ends with these lines:

> These became part of that child who went forth every day,
> and who now goes, and will always go forth every day.

These final lines capture the spirit of a process understanding of human life. We are "always going forth" every day. What we experience, what happens to us, and how we respond to what happens to us, make us who we are. Our being is our becoming.

Of course, the idea that being is becoming is not at all unique to the West. Long before Walt Whitman, the *Analects* of Confucius expressed a similar idea in its proposal that the process of learning how to live is a lifelong process. In the *Analects* we read:

> At fifteen I set my heart upon learning. At thirty, I had planted my feet upon firm ground. At forty, I no longer suffered from perplexities. At fifty, I knew what were the biddings of Heaven. At sixty, I heard them with a docile ear. At seventy, I could follow the dictates of my own heart for what I desired no longer overstepped the boundaries of right.

Confucius did not feel that he was fully mature until he was very old. Process philosophers agree with Walt Whitman and Confucius. They believe that life is a process and that creative transformation— moment by moment—is what life is all about.

THE FALLACY OF STAGNANT HARMONY

The fallacy of stagnant harmony is a phrase I use to capture another important part of process thinking. The fallacy lies in thinking that if some harmony has been achieved in life—a stable relation between human beings, for example—that harmony must forever remain fixed and changeless because it is perfect as it is. When people fall victim to this fallacy, they lapse into a false view of virtue and perfection. They think that virtue is solid and rigid like a rock, not realizing that it is creative and adaptive like a river. A process point of view offers a more dynamic understanding of harmony as harmony in-process. This kind of harmony can include novelty and openness to creative transformation.

It is especially important for highly idealistic people to avoid this fallacy, because in their idealism to create a more just society or a more peaceful society, they can fall into the view that their particular image of that society is absolute and that the reality for which they hope, once achieved, will be permanent. When people avoid the fallacy of stagnant harmony, they realize that even their best laid plans will be subject to change and that life goes on without them. They learn to seek harmony *and* expect change, cognizant that harmony is itself changing.

THE FALLACY OF MISDIRECTED CREATIVITY

The fallacy of misdirected creativity lies in thinking that the adventurous and creative side of life can be fully satisfied by service to the ego. This is especially prominent in an age of consumerism, where people measure their own worth and that of others by standards of appearance, affluence, and marketable achievement, and where market-driven values such as competition and individualism often override more social values such as cooperation and service. When people fall into this fallacy, they think of themselves as skin-encased egos, cut off from the world by the boundaries of their skin, forgetting that they are persons-in-community whose happiness depends on, and can contribute to, the happiness of others. A more relational understanding of creativity becomes obvious when we think of people who use their creativity toward ends that help others and make a constructive contribution to the world. Even as personal happiness may not be their conscious aim, they are often happier than more self-centered people. Their happiness is a byproduct of their receptivity to the feelings of others and their desire to help them. Once their own needs for survival are met, they want to help others and build compassionate communities. They avoid the fallacy of misdirected creativity.

THE FALLACY OF HARMONY WITHOUT DIFFERENCES

This fallacy has three aspects. One is the fallacy of thinking that, by virtue of cultural or ideological differences, people cannot share in one another's sufferings and joys, because the gaps between them are insurmountable. The second lies in thinking that, if people share in one another's suffering and joys, their differences are therefore eliminated. And the third is that, if differences remain, there is a problem, because diversity is inherently divisive. Out of this concern to avoid divisive diversity, people fall into the fallacy of seeking a kind of harmony in which there are no differences and no tensions whatsoever.

To be sure, some forms of diversity are divisive. When people are at war with each other, there is divisive diversity. But from a process point of view, many forms of diversity are quite desirable. Harmony is not sameness, and sometimes harmony between people includes and even needs tensions. Good friends, for example, need not agree with one another in order to care for each other and dwell in harmony with one another. Their disagreements can be part of the harmony of their relationship. The same situation applies between cultures, organizations, groups, and nations. Harmony can include healthy competition.

The alternative to the fallacy of harmony without difference is to embrace what Wang Zhihe calls a philosophy of Harmonism, which is harmony with differences. The spirit of Harmonism welcomes differences and is simultaneously open to cross-cultural communication and interreligious dialogue. It is facilitated by several ideas in Whitehead's thought.

One is Whitehead's understanding of the *imagination*. He believes that it is possible for people to imagine themselves inside the shoes of others, even if they have not shared a common past, because certain potentialities for feeling, embodied in the other, can be imagined by the person who does not share the other's past. This capacity to imagine other shoes is commonplace among actors; Whitehead's philosophy suggests that ordinary people, too, can partake of this capacity.

Another idea is Whitehead's notion of *hybrid prehensions*, amid which a person can "feel the feelings" of others, even if those feelings do not belong to him or her. For example, when a person walks into a room we can often sense the mood of that person even if the person does not directly communicate that mood. In English, we say that a person comes into a room and "lights up the room" because her mood is energetic or joyful; and also that a person comes into a room and "darkens the atmosphere," because the person is angry with others in the room. These colloquialisms point to the common reality that people feel the feelings of others and are shaped by those feelings.

A third aspect of Whitehead's thought that supports a philosophy of Harmonism is Whitehead's notion that the *unity of the universe is itself enriched by diversity itself.* In *For the Common Good,* John Cobb and Herman Daly speak of this unity as the Sacred Whole. It is the whole of the universe as the widest and most inclusive whole imaginable, which itself can be impoverished by a diminution of diversity and enriched by an addition of diversity. Whitehead spoke of this whole as God. As noted earlier, God in Whitehead is not external to the whole of the universe, God is the whole of the universe as a living whole in which diversity adds to the life of God.

THE FALLACY OF THE PERFECT DICTIONARY

This is the fallacy of reducing our understanding of the world to sets of definitions drawn from the dictionary. First, it neglects the fact that every event in the world is a creative synthesis of an infinite number of connections and thus that all definitions are abstractions from the concrete. Second, it neglects the fact that dictionary definitions are themselves the product of historical processes and that the very meanings of words can change over time. And third, it neglects the fact that even abstract ideas—Whitehead calls them propositions—are not reducible to their linguistic expressions.

One alternative to the fallacy of the perfect dictionary is to recognize that verbal language itself is inexact and context-based, and that sometimes novel forms of language—metaphors, for example—can better express certain ideas than more rarefied forms of abstract language. Another alternative is to recognize that sometimes ideas can be better presented, or at least as ably presented, through the arts and other forms of communication than through verbal language.

With regard to philosophy, the biologist Charles Birch offers an excellent description: "The fallacy of the perfect dictionary divides philosophy, said Whitehead, into two schools; the critical school and the speculative school. The critical school confines itself to verbal analysis within the limits of the dictionary. The speculative school enlarges the dictionary by exploring meanings and seeking further insights. It is willing to have an attitude of adventure in the face of mystery and ignorance. The divergence between the two is, suggests Whitehead, the quarrel between safety and adventure."[10]

THE FALLACY OF SIMPLE LOCATION

This is the fallacy of thinking that a given event in the universe—a human action, an atomic event—is simply located in one region and not also located in others. The problem of assuming simple location follows from Whitehead's analysis of experience.

For purposes of illustration, imagine a mother sharing a meal with her daughter. Whitehead was interested in the question: *Where* is she? At one level the mother is located where she is sitting, in the chair on the left side of the table. But as she listens to her daughter, the mother's attention is directed to the other side of the table, where her daughter is sitting. Phenomenologically, the mother is "over there" where her daughter is, even as she is also "right here" where she is sitting. A scientist might trace this to signals that are transmitted from her daughter to her eyes and ears, and then say that the whole experience is occurring inside her brain, which does seem to be "simply located" in her body. And yet, even if her daughter is truly on the other side of the table, and information is transmitted from daughter to mother, there must be something about the daughter—some aspect of the daughter's existence—that was once part of the daughter and is now inside the brain of the mother. We call this something *information* about the daughter. This means that the daughter "over there" is again "right here" where the mother is sitting. Thus, to the question "Where is the mother?," we must say: "She is where she is sitting in some ways, but she is also in other locations, too, albeit less directly." We begin to see the mother's own existence as more like a field than a particle: a field of awareness that may be centered in a region but reaches out beyond that region to include and be affected by others.

For process thinkers, it is important to avoid the fallacy of simple location for ethical reasons. The fallacy reminds us that we ourselves cannot assume simple location, and thus that our experience and our actions have a ripple effect in the world, sometimes with consequences that extend far beyond our immediate horizons. These horizons are both spatial and temporal. As temporal, they include the future. Some process thinkers suggest that, if we want to act responsibly in the present, we must commit ourselves to a constructively postmodern future that is healthy for all people, and simultaneously builds upon the best of the past.

Why Do Some People Speak of Process Thought as "Constructive Postmodernism"?

Constructive postmodernism is a new phrase to many people, and it is often confused with deconstructive postmodernism. For process thinkers, the two are quite different. The particular thinker who has used the phrase constructive postmodernism most often is David Ray Griffin, especially in his series on Constructive Postmodern Thought published by the State University of New York Press. Some process thinkers in China and other parts of the world find value in Griffin's phrase; others do not. Those who avoid the phrase usually do so because they believe that the word postmodernism is inescapably tied to the deconstructive postmodern movement of Europe, as articulated by thinkers such as Jacques Derrida (1930–2005), Michel Foucault (1926–1984), Julia Kristeva (b. 1941), Jacques Lacan (1901–1981), Emmanuel Levinas (1906–1995), and Jean-Francois Lyotard (1924–1998). Deconstructive postmodern thinkers have a wide array of emphases, and there is no simple way to categorize them in a single paragraph. They variously emphasize the role of ideology in human discourse: the way in which human subjectivity is constructed out of linguistic signs and symbols; the homogenizing nature of all meta-narratives; the value of cultural pluralism.

In varying degrees and ways, all process thinkers are sympathetic to these emphases. From a Whiteheadian perspective it is certainly true that all language, including Whiteheadian language, has ideological implications. Language can reveal and conceal aspects of the world and human experience; it can promote or challenge the interests of the dominant social and economic class. From a Whiteheadian perspective it is also true that human subjectivity, while not reducible to linguistic experience, is profoundly shaped by that experience. When human beings say words like "I" and "We" their very understandings of "I" and "We" are influenced by what those words mean in advertisements, books, and movies. The "I" that is spoken by a teenager deeply influenced by celebrity culture is not the same "I" that is spoken by a monk in a monastery, and their experience differs as well.

From a Whiteheadian perspective, it is also true that synoptic visions of the world and human life—including the process vision—can function to reduce diversity to sameness, under the lens of a false homogenizing of different and disparate realities. When this happens, they should be critiqued. And from a Whiteheadian perspective, it is true that sometimes human beings need novelty in life, even when it destabilizes existing forms of order. It is in this spirit of appreciating the value of the deconstructive movement, then, that Whiteheadians also point beyond it. They believe that deconstructive philosophies do not go far enough, because they typically stop at criticizing modernity and modern societies, without offering a constructive vision in its place. This gets to a practical and pragmatic side of the process tradition. It is not simply interested in metaphysics; it is interested in reducing suffering in human life and helping people become free and happy. In short, the process tradition is interested in what people call the common good and in constructive alternatives to the many problems societies face today. A constructively postmodern approach to life has two important qualities. First, it builds upon the best of modern, industrial ways of thinking, while critiquing the worst of those ways of thinking. Second, it appropriates the best of more traditional or premodern ways of thinking, while critiquing the worst of these ways.

Of course, phrases such as "modern" and "premodern" also require critique, especially insofar as they can function as ways of fostering images of human development that necessarily follow a Western, industrial path. From the perspective of an organic farmer in China who does not use herbicides or pesticides, there is nothing "premodern" about his method farming; rather, there is something deeply unsustainable about more "modern" forms of farming that denude topsoil and release chemicals into underground water supplies. Nevertheless, even as terms such as "premodern" and "modern" can be quite packed with problematic assumptions, they are used in different parts of the world in helpful ways, so I will use them, too.

When process philosophies claim to be "constructively post-modern," they have in mind building upon the best of modernity and also avoiding the worst, while reclaiming the wisdom of pre-industrial and more traditional ways of living. They believe that people can be "modern" and "scientific" and "rational" in the best of modern ways. But they also believe that people can be appreciative of tradition, respectful of cultural diversity, grateful for the role of community in human life, respectful of the Earth, open to the best of religious wisdom, and sensitive to the wisdom of the arts and other forms of aesthetic wisdom.

How Can Process
Thought Be Practiced?

For process thinkers, this is the most important question, because theory and practice cannot be separated. People's ideas are shaped by their practices, and their practices are shaped by their ideas. In more technical terms, Whiteheadians believe that theory and practice cannot be separated for two reasons.

First, every moment of human experience involves receiving influences from other realities and influencing them in some way. We might call it the "yin" and "yang" of human experience. We are always affecting and being affected by the world. To pretend that we can rest in pure theory without affecting and being affected by others is pure illusion.

Second, the mental side of life is incomplete and deficient in actuality unless completed by the physical side of life. Whitehead speaks of the mental side as the "mental pole" of experience and the physical side as the "physical pole," and indicates that they dwell in deep relation with one another. The mental pole would be that side of our lives in which we theorize about the world. The physical pole would be that side by which the world shapes us and enters into our own experience through experience in the mode of causal efficacy. There would be nothing to theorize about were there not a world presented to experience about which one could theorize. Again, we might speak of this as the "yin" and "yang" of experience.

Whitehead further suggests that these yin-yang dynamics are found throughout the whole of nature so that the human need to complement theory with practice is rooted in the fundamental dynamics of the cosmos. Even the Heaven in Whitehead's philosophy—even God—needs a world in order to be actual. Even Heaven cannot live by theory alone. Life is a whole.

What, then, are ways of practicing process thought? In a very general way, we might say that any human activity that helps create and sustain human wholeness within the larger context of sustainable community is a process practice. In this chapter, I want to emphasize (1) the lifestyle to which process thought points, (2) ethical guidelines for responsible decision making, (3) individual practices aimed at personal well-being and spiritual health, and (4) shared rituals aimed at sustainable community.

A PROCESS LIFESTYLE: LIVING THE VIRTUOUS LIFE

In order to approach the question of lifestyle, it is helpful to recall the ancient adage that, in order for people to live healthy lives, they need roots and wings. "Roots" is a metaphor for the security and balance that people enjoy when they live in healthy communities, have healthy family relations, and feel grounded in the best of their cultural traditions. "Wings" is a metaphor for the sense of happiness people enjoy when they can be open to new experiences, new insights, and different kinds of people. The lifestyle recommended by process thought has roots and wings. The problem in modern times, though, is that many people feel torn between two undesirable options: a rootless consumerism that is exciting but lacks balance, and a wingless traditionalism that focuses on the past at the expense of being open to the future.

Rootless consumerism is very different from healthy consumption.[11] Healthy consumption is the enjoyment of goods and services that are produced and consumed in environmentally benign ways, that free people from drudgery so that their lives can be easier, and that enrich the body and mind. The fruits of creative consumption are good food, comfortable shelter, attractive clothing, quality health care, and enjoyable forms of recreation, made possible by satisfying jobs and quality education. Some of these fruits are necessary for survival, and all contribute to happiness in life. It is a tragedy that too many in the world suffer from its absence: poverty, disease, unemployment, drudgery, and a sense of helplessness.[12]

Rootless consumerism is a cultural atmosphere that emerges in a society when it is saturated with market-driven values such as competition and a preoccupation with status, and when other more social values such as compassion and sharing fall away. Some of its tangible effects are conspicuous consumption, wasteful consumption, and over-consumption. But these tangible effects are mere symptoms of a deeper philosophy of life that can overwhelm an individual and permeate a society. Rootless consumerism is this philosophy of life. It tells people that they are fulfilled or made whole by purchasing more and more consumer goods each year without ever having to say "enough." It teaches them to measure their own worth by how attractive they are by consumer-driven standards; by how much money they have; and by how much status they have in terms of the goods they own. Rootless consumerism tells them that they are consumers first and citizens second, such that their private good is more important than the public good. It tells them that paid jobs are more important than their families, and that paid work is the only work worth doing. It says life is a race toward material success, in which there must be winners and losers. When market-driven values such as these dominate a society, things fall apart. Being ambitious becomes more important than being good; being attractive becomes more important than being kind; being materially successful becomes more important than being a good parent, neighbor, and friend. People are more interested in new clothes than old friends. The social costs of consumerism are excessive individualism, a neglect of family and community, an overemphasis on money, a compulsively busy lifestyle, and a sense of emptiness that comes when life is reduced to things.

Wingless traditionalism is equally pernicious. When people are trapped in the atmosphere of wingless traditionalism, they are afraid of novelty and surprise and anything that seems unfamiliar because they are clinging to what is familiar to them. Often they cling to a religious or political ideology or to ethnic traditions, and they become so attached to that ideology that they develop an unhealthy fear of anyone who lies outside the boundaries of their own "in group." They cannot think in wider and more inclusive terms. They become slaves to familiar comforts at the expense of welcoming strangers. Sometimes they resort to violence to settle disputes, at the expense of entering into open dialogue. In rootless consumerism there are wings without roots; in wingless traditionalism there are roots without wings. Many people turn to rootless consumerism as the only available alternative to a wingless traditionalism. They reject the dominant ideology of their time and make consumption their religion. In doing so, they lose some roots but gain some wings.

Process thought points toward a creative alternative to rootless consumerism and wingless traditionalism. In the first chapter of this book, I called it *creative harmony*. The word "creative" is used to name a way of living that is open to new ideas and possibilities. The word "harmony" is used to name a sense of living in sympathetic coordination with other people, other living beings, and the deeper rhythms of the universe.

Creative harmony might also be understood by borrowing a term from Chinese culture, *wu-wei*. Creative harmony is a *creative, postmodern wu-wei.* Traditionally, *wu-wei* refers to a way of living that is attuned to the deeper rhythms and norms of the universe and that acts out of that attunement rather than out of more ego-based or self-centered approaches to life. Creative harmony is like this. It is a practical and spiritually meaningful way of living that is available to people from many different cultures and all walks of life. Businessmen and farmers, schoolteachers and architects, poets and engineers—all have their way of living in a spirit of creative harmony. It is not a path to be traveled by all people in exactly the same way, but is instead a way of walking that can accommodate many different paths. It is flexible and adaptive rather than fixed and rigid.

People who embody this way of living do not need to feel special and privileged. They are not trying to climb a ladder of upward mobility in which others are left behind; instead, they put the ladder on its side. They see the adventurous side of life as a growth in the quality of relationships, not a growth in individual prosperity. They can be ambitious, but they are not blinded by their ambition. They want to make enough money to live comfortably, to enjoy the companionship of family and friends, to enjoy opportunities for leisure, and to enjoy meaningful work. But they will also care about the natural world and about people whom the rest of society might sometimes neglect: people at the dawn of life (children), people in the twilight of life (the elderly), and people in the shadows of life, including the poor, the sick, and the needy. Thus they will not seek happiness only for themselves. They will seek it for all people and for all living beings. At an ethical level, then, they live with respect and care for the entire community of life. At a social level they seek to help build sustainable communities. And at a spiritual level they will try to live in harmony with the deeper rhythms of the universe itself. They may speak of this harmony with the deeper rhythms of the universe as "trust in the Dao" or "faith in God" or "harmony with the whole." Whatever phrases they use, the fruits of their efforts will be similar. Their gods will be compassion, not indifference; respect, not disdain; humility, not vanity; joy, not greed.

ETHICAL GUIDELINES FOR RESPONSIBLE DECISION-MAKING

Of course, a practice of process thought cannot rely on virtue alone. It will also need guidelines for ethical behavior. For most process thinkers, these guidelines do not come simply from a deductive approach by which they are logically derived from process thought without reference to context. Rather, and perhaps most importantly, they come by consensus, through consultations with people in different parts of the world who jointly hope for the kinds of sustainable communities to which process thought points. Such an approach would be consistent with process thought, which generally emphasizes grassroots approaches over top-down approaches.

There is a set of principles that was developed in this consultative way, and it matches the general orientation of most process thinkers in different parts of the world. These are the principles of the Earth Charter, and they function as good examples of the kinds of principles to which process thought points. (See Appendix F.) For a complete understanding, readers should look up the subprinciples at *earthcharter.org*. These subprinciples give greater specificity to each of the principles and offer more practical guidelines for application, but even the general principles offer helpful direction.

Each of these principles has implications for important issues faced by society today. Consider Principle 11, which insists upon universal access to healthcare, education, and employment. In many nations in the world today, including the United States, the wealthier people have access to healthcare that others lack, and poor people lack health security in a variety of ways. Following the guidelines of the Earth Charter, a process approach would aim at equity in healthcare and the availability of universal healthcare. It would also support actions undertaken on the part of governments to ensure full employment for all people and equal access to quality education.

Consider also Principle 6, which is sometimes called the precautionary principle. This principle says that if an action or policy is being considered by an organization, and that this action might cause severe and irreversible damage to the public, then, in the absence of scientific consensus that it will not cause harm, those who advocate taking the action bear the burden of proof. The precautionary principle has implications for biotechnologies. For example, the precautionary principle leads process thinkers to reject human cloning and reject proposals for social eugenics. Cloning would raise serious complications for family life. As one leading process thinker, Ian Barbour, puts it: "Should a cloned child from a woman be viewed as her daughter—or her delayed twin sister?"[13] How would this confusion about her identity affect the child? Should she think of herself as her mother's daughter or her mother's sister?

With regard to other forms of genetic modification, process thinkers *cautiously* accept somatic cell gene therapy for genetic defects. Such therapy modifies genes in human beings that are not reproductive in nature, thus affecting future generations, but that can relieve suffering from painful diseases. But process thinkers warn against germline therapies aimed at reducing genetic defects in future generations. For example, Barbour accepts germline therapies only under three "precautionary" conditions.[14]

First, extensive tests must be made on somatic cells that may be indirectly affected by germline therapies; second, extensive tests over long periods of time must be followed over several generations to assure the reliability and long-term effects are safe; and third, widespread public support must be gained. Barbour recommends that governmental agencies and research organizations adopt these policies. This policy would be one practical outcome of practicing process thought at the level of public policy.

INDIVIDUAL PRACTICES:
PERSONAL WELL-BEING AND SPIRITUAL HEALTH

In the West today there is a great deal of emphasis on personal wholeness. People want and seek to be whole persons; that is, to live with a sense of having an inner source of freshness and renewal that can help them get through stressful situations and give them a sense of creativity in daily life. Toward this end, some process thinkers recommend individual practices, undertaken on a daily basis, aimed at personal well-being and spiritual health.

There is not a single practice that process thinkers might recommend, because different cultures and different traditions offer different options. In China, for example, a daily practice of tai chi chuan would be one example of a daily practice; among Christians and Buddhists in different parts of the world, a daily practice of prayer and meditation. What a process thinker might add, though, is that a key is regularity and consistency, so that a person finds a way of being composed and creative in daily life. The intentions that a person brings to the daily practice would also be important; Whitehead speaks of intentions as subjective aims. In the experience of many people in different parts of the world, a daily practice of one sort or another provides a sense of anchorage and balance that can then ripple out into the day.

Process thought is especially helpful in understanding the

importance of the body in daily, individual practices. In process thought, the mind and body are closely connected, each affecting the other. This means that a person's attitudes toward life and general sense of confidence and well-being can be enriched by bodily exercise and traditional spiritual disciplines that involve the body. Such practices can help "center" persons and give them a sense of inner peace and calm in daily life, helping them become more creative, less impulsive, more relaxed, and better able to accept the ups and downs of a given day.

Process thinkers have also developed various understandings of prayer. In historical traditions throughout the world, there are many kinds of prayer. These include prayers of thanksgiving, prayers of contemplation, prayers of petition, and prayers of confession. Sometimes they use words, but also rituals, such as the lighting of incense before the statue of a Buddha. They can also be danced or simply felt, without the use of words at all. For many process thinkers these activities make good sense, because there is indeed a Harmony of Harmonies embracing the universe that can both receive the prayers and respond to them.

Finally, daily spiritual practices can include simple reflective reading, such as reading inspirational literature, passages from poetry, or from classic cultural and spiritual texts such as the Dao de Ching, the Bible, the Bhagavad Gita, or the Qu'ran. There is not a single canon of reading to which process thinkers point. The Harmony of Harmonies can find itself into a person's life in myriad ways. The key is to have some kind of daily practice that seeks to be open to that Harmony.

SHARED RITUALS: COMMUNITY PRACTICES
FOR SUSTAINABLE COMMUNITY

At the level of social practices, there are many ways to practice process thought. Recall the definition of sustainable community offered above. It is a community that is creative, compassionate, equitable, ecologically wise, respectful of diversity, scientifically informed, and spiritually satisfying—with no one left behind. Any practice adopted by individuals or groups that contributes to the nourishment of such communities would be a way of practicing process thought.

Sometimes these practices are indistinguishable from cultural customs. For example, the enjoyment of food at a common table—where friends and family members are gathered together—would be a kind of process practice. Here we would see a living example of creativity in the preparing and sharing of the food, and also of spiritual satisfaction in the enjoyment of relations within the group. When a stranger is brought in and also welcomed at the table, there is a widening of harmony amid the practice. There would be an added component of respect for diversity. And if the food happens to be healthy, the very selection of it would be a way of practicing ecological wisdom.

Another example of a social practice would be participation in group settings, where all are allowed to speak and deliberate together, without fear of expressing their opinions. In the United States, for example, there is a tradition of town hall meetings where citizens in a given community get together to address a common concern, and it often includes healthy debate. This would be a practice that embodies participation.

Still another example of a social practice would be volunteer work aimed at helping people who are poor or sick, young or old. The spirit of volunteerism that has been an important part of American life is one instance of this, and often it has been organized through churches, synagogues, and mosques, sometimes together. For example, Habitat for Humanity brings people together to build houses for others, and often these "builds" involve participation of people from different religions. Thus people of faith practice helping others—making sure that no one is left behind—and at the same time they practice respect for diversity, in this case inter-religious diversity.

An additional social practice appreciated by process thinkers would be communal enjoyment of the arts and of beauty. This, too, from a process perspective, is part of spiritual satisfaction in life. For process thinkers, the very aim of life is to enjoy harmony and intensity, one word for which is "beauty." The collective enjoyment of creative and performing arts is a way that people feel bonds with one another.

By way of concluding this section on shared practices, then, I offer one last example: the Green Biking movement. This is an interesting practice because it integrates so many features of sustainable community: physical health, bondedness with others, and protection of the Earth. Biking can seem old-fashioned. And yet, in light of global warming, bicycling is not simply an old-fashioned way of moving from one location to another, but a forward-looking and still more modern way of moving by virtue of its health benefits and benefit to the environment. If riding in cars is modern, then riding on bikes is constructively postmodern.

Process thought seeks to build upon the past, point toward the future, care for the Earth, care for people, and add beauty to the world. This book began with the image of process thought as a bridge-building tradition. It rightly ends with the idea that people can ride bicycles across the bridges, too. Riding bicycles is a physical activity in its own right and also a metaphor for the many practical ways in which process thought can be practiced.

The deepest commitment of process thought is toward a way of living in the world that embodies respect and care for the community of life. Certainly, some of this respect and care can come about with help from theories in process thought. But still more can come about when people put those ideas into practice. Riding bikes, volunteering time to help others, encouraging creativity in children, sharing meals with friends, developing businesses that help the Earth and people, spending time in prayer or meditation, planting a garden, making tough decisions on matters of bioethics, participating in civic discussion, learning a new language—all of these, in proper context, are ways of practicing process thought. All are part of the world's best hope.

Appendices

Appendix A:
The Rational Life in
Whiteheadian Perspective

Harmony is a key word in Whitehead. He believes that human beings aim at harmony, that living cells aim at harmony, that molecules and atoms aim at harmony, and that the universe as a whole aims at harmony. Whitehead speaks of a divine reality which is a Harmony of Harmonies. Always, what he has in mind is a dynamic harmony, a creative harmony. It is a harmony in process, in which there is openness to what is new and different. In human life, for example, people *rightly* desire to live in harmony with one another and with the natural world. I say rightly, because, in fact, humans do not always feel this desire or act on it. There is much injustice in the world, much environmental neglect, much callousness. But process thinkers believe that, deep within each human being, there is a desire to live in harmony with one another and with the surrounding world, even if this desire is covered over by other concerns or intentionally neglected. However, the harmony that humans appropriately seek is not a static harmony that lacks intensity or vitality, novelty or surprise. It is not a harmony where everything remains the same and nothing ever changes. It is instead a dynamic harmony that is creative and open, perpetually available to new possibilities.

Human reason, then, is one way that people seek this creative harmony. Rational understanding is itself a kind of harmony, a kind of rapport with the surrounding world. When we think about reason in this way, reason is not simply instrumental reason. It is not reducible to a calculation of effective means to deal with arbitrarily chosen ends, such as maximizing profit or aggrandizing the ego or seeking security. The aim of reason is wisdom, and wisdom lies in understanding various aspects of the world experienced—plants and animals, for example, and human communities—but also in seeing these things in their connections. "The task of reason," says Whitehead in *Process and Reality,* "is to fathom the deeper depths of the many-sidedness of things" (342).

The process of fathoming the depths and many-sidedness of things involves calculation, intuition, imagination, and attention to what is experienced in the here and now of daily life. In *Process and Reality* Whitehead puts it this way:

> Our datum is the actual world, including ourselves; and this actual world spreads itself for observation in the guise of the topic of our immediate experience. The elucidation of immediate experience is the sole justification for any thought; and the starting point is the analytic observation of components of this experience. (4)

This passage points to the empirical side of Whitehead's thought. When Whitehead says that our topic is the actual world which spreads itself out in the guise of the topic of our immediate experience, he means that human experience itself, in the present moment, is an act of being in the world, and that the world cannot be separated from experience. In *Modes of Thought* he says: "We are in the world and the world is in us" (165). For him this does not mean that the world is a projection of our imaginations; it means instead that every moment of experience begins with an act of receiving the world and being affected by it. Whitehead speaks of this as the "givenness" of the world to be experienced. The world consists of "stubborn facts that cannot be evaded" (PR 43).

This idea of the givenness of the world—of stubborn facts—is not in fashion in certain circles of philosophy today. Many post-modern philosophies in the West highlight the role that human beings play in constructing their world. By this they mean that the world humans experience is inevitably interpreted through systems of signs and symbols. Whitehead would agree. But he also thinks that there is something given in each moment of experience that cannot be reduced to signs and symbols: the air we breathe, the food we eat, the pleasures and pains we feel in our bodies, the faces of other people, the plants and animals and mountains. Philosophy must make sense of the givenness of the world.

Of course, even as Whitehead was an empiricist, he was also a rationalist. The philosophy he developed was intended to "have its rational side and its empirical side" (PR 3). He was a mathematician for much of his life, and he was at home in the world of intellectual abstractions, concerned with the avoidance of contradictions, and following the rules of inference. His earliest works were in algebra, geometry, and symbolic logic. He brought this interest in logic to his more mature philosophy. Whitehead believed that, in framing a set of ideas, a philosopher needs to make sure the ideas are coherent and logical (PR 3). If the universe is a coherent whole in which everything is interconnected, then the coherence of ideas in a philosophical system is a way of appreciating this inter-connectedness. Most process thinkers think of Whitehead as trying to balance the rationalist and empirical approach to philosophy: "the two sides are bound together" (PR 3).

Nevertheless, Whitehead was fully aware that philosophers can create systems of ideas that are remarkable in their rational coherence and logical consistency, but do not speak to the concreteness of human experience as it unfolds in history. They are perfect "systems" but lack contact with the world. They do not appeal to the evidence of experience itself (AI 226). Thus he advocated what we might call a deep empiricism, in which the entire range of experience is included. In philosophy, he says:

> Nothing can be omitted, experience drunk and experience sober, experience sleeping and experience waking, experience drowsy and experience wide-awake, experience self-conscious and experience self-forgetful, experience intellectual and experience physical, experience religious and experience skeptical, experience anxious and experience care-free, experience anticipatory and experience grieving, experience dominated by emotion and experience under self-restraint, experience in the light and experience in the dark, experience normal and experience abnormal. (AI 226)

The passage reveals something essential to Whitehead: He does not believe human experience is restricted to sense-perception. Human experience includes what happens to people when they sleep, when they have religious feelings, when they undergo powerful emotions, when they feel confused, when they feel skeptical, when they remember the past, when they anticipate the future, when they think scientifically, when they feel beauty. For Whitehead, all of these experiences tell us something about ourselves, and many of them tell us something about the universe. This is why, when he began to develop his worldview, he sought to integrate insights that emerge from different kinds of human experience: scientific, aesthetic, moral, and spiritual.

Science was very important to Whitehead. He spent forty years as a philosopher of science and a mathematician before turning in a professional way to philosophy. One of the great strengths of his philosophy is that it is scientifically informed. But science was not the only source of knowledge. Aesthetic, moral, and spiritual experiences were also important—and they could be part of what he called a rational approach to the world. Science provides insights into that side of reality that is subject to mathematical analysis and repeatable experimentation. Moral intuitions provide insight into that side of reality that people experience within themselves when they feel inwardly beckoned to share in the destinies of others; and when they recognize that other human beings are subjects of their own lives, deserving respect in their own right. Aesthetics provides insights into that side of reality which is beautiful to behold and, still more deeply, to that side of reality that people experience within themselves as they feel inwardly drawn to live in harmony with the surrounding world. And religion provides insight into that side of reality by which people feel beckoned by a higher power, a deeper self, or the sheer connectedness of things. Of course these "sides of reality" are not sharply separated. The power of Whitehead is that he unites these sensibilities with a deep appreciation of science.

Appendix B:
Culture—Propositions—
Education

IN A WHITEHEADIAN CONTEXT, a culture can be defined in material and axiological terms. It consists of the built environments in which people dwell, and it includes their modes of production. Culture also consists of the values and ideals to which they subscribe. Whiteheadians will insist that these two dimensions of a culture—the material and the axiological—have a reciprocal relation. How people think and what they value affects how they live; and how they live affects how they think. I use the term *cultural atmosphere* to refer to the first side of the equation: how people think and what they value. I presuppose that such an atmosphere is not an island unto itself. Like all realities, a cultural atmosphere is shaped by modes of production. For example, if people live in a rural area and find themselves laboring each day without the benefits of labor-saving technologies, the very drudgery of their work will shape their cultural atmosphere. They will be tired. And if they feel beholden to authorities who do not allow them the fruits of their labors, this power relation will likewise shape their culture. Their cultural atmosphere will include a hidden sense of resentment. This is one reason why, among Whiteheadians, rural development is so important. One problem with Western modernity is that it overemphasized urban development at the expense of rural development. The need is for the two to develop in tandem with one another, where rural peoples enjoy a rich quality of life, not feeling the need to migrate to cities. A constructive postmodern culture will include constructively postmodern *rural* living.

In a Whiteheadian context, a cultural *atmosphere* is a set of moods, desires, and attitudes that are shared by people and transmitted through various forms of education. In the language of Whitehead, they are *subjective forms* (moods) and *subjective aims* (desires) and *metaphysical perspectives* (outlooks on life) to which people consciously or unconsciously adhere. These moods, desires, and outlooks shape the way people feel the presence of other people and the surrounding world, and they influence how people creatively respond to other people and the surrounding world.

For the moment, I am using the word education very broadly. I am referring to the development of outlooks on life, desires, and moods that emerge in a person's life, as he or she has experiences at home, in the workplace, in public schools, and in community life. These developments are both intellectual and emotional; a Whiteheadian will not sharply distinguish between the intellectual and affective side of life. The developments occur through oral conversations, friendships, experiences in life, books, television, movies, music, and advertisements. Given this notion of education, we must note that, in modern society, many young people are educated, not simply by what they learn in the classroom, but also, and sometimes more deeply, by what they hear in popular music, what their friends are doing, and what they see their parents doing. Movie stars are their teachers; popular music is their bible. Understood in this very general way, education can be healthy or unhealthy. It is the means by which cultural atmospheres emerge and change over time.

Cultural atmospheres, too, can be healthy or unhealthy. If a young boy is born into a cultural atmosphere that valorizes violence, for example, this violence is something into which he is thrown at birth and for which he cannot be held responsible. He finds himself wanting to be violent, too, if only to survive in the presence of others who are violent. From a Whiteheadian perspective, an overly violent cultural atmosphere is unhealthy, but quite powerful. It has intensity without harmony, except for the harmony experienced within an in-group that develops its sense of identity by demonizing an out-group. One problem in the world today is that too many people are born into cultures—some of them religiously inspired— that valorize violence over dialogue.

Of course, people cannot be reduced to their cultures. They are also shaped by their genes and body chemistry and by the personal decisions they have made in their lives or are making. They are responsible for their actions; they cannot simply say "my culture made me do it," or "my body made me do it." But one's culture does indeed play a tremendously important role in these decisions for good or ill. All human life is culturally conditioned and culturally shaped. Equally important, cultures can themselves be further shaped by people who live within them. Cultures can be transformed. Of course, cultures can be transformed in many ways. A natural disaster or war can transform a culture; a change in political leadership can transform a culture. But another way that cultures get transformed is by means of novel ideas that are discovered or created by their participants. This raises the question: What is an *idea*?

In Whitehead's thought, an idea is called a *proposition*. The word can be misleading, because a proposition is not a linguistic entity or a verbal expression. Most of the propositions that shape our lives are never articulated in language; instead they reside within us as deeply felt intuitions, hopes, and dreams. For example, when a young child who has not developed language is hungry, the child has the idea: "I want food." But the child does not have the language to express the idea, so the child cries instead. The crying becomes a means to expressing the idea. Even more abstract ideas, such as "everything is in process" or "everything is interconnected" can be felt, even if a person lacks words to clearly articulate them. Indeed, even mathematical ideas are not reducible to the symbolic means by which they are expressed. The multiplication table up to twelve can be articulated in many different languages and written signs, but the table itself is more than its articulations. Whitehead suggests that the table itself resides in a realm of pure potentiality that is not inherently linguistic but that can nevertheless be intellectually apprehended: "We must admit that in some sense or other, we inevitably presuppose this realm of forms, in abstraction from loss or gain. For example, the multiplication table up to 'twelve times twelve' is a humble member of it" (MT 68).

A proposition, then, may pertain to intellectual abstractions, physically felt goals, universal truths, or particular situations. Indeed, Whitehead believes that people can apprehend propositions unconsciously as well as consciously. When people dream, they may experience various ideas, albeit of a semiconscious nature. Most generally, a proposition is an inwardly felt idea or proposal for how we might live in the world. It is a proposal or a "lure for feeling," which may or may not include a claim to literal, sensory-perceived facts (PR 25). For example, when a person tells a joke, he or she is articulating an idea, a proposition. But the idea is not meant to be true in a literal sense. We cannot and need not photograph its content, because the content is invisible to the eye, yet felt in the minds of the one telling the joke and the ones who are listening. A proposition is meant to evoke a form of consciousness in the listener. Whitehead is quite interested in true propositions, but he is also famous for insisting that even true propositions are not reducible to their linguistic expres sions: "It is merely credulous to accept verbal statements as adequate expressions of propositions" (PR 11). And he is famous for saying that, in many circumstance, it is more important that a proposition be interesting than that it be true (PR 259). A joke would be an example of propositions that are interesting, and thereby rich in value, but not literally true. Still more deeply, Whitehead believed that many religious propositions have their final value, not because they are literally true or false in a scientific sense, but because they evoke various forms of "aesthetic delight" that reveal the deeper wisdom of life (PR 185). This means that, for Whitehead, much religion is, and ought to be understood as, metaphorical. To repeat: a proposition is a "lure for feeling."

In the English language, the word *lure* can refer to something that is deceptive or seductive; or it can simply refer to something that has attractive power. Whitehead uses the word in the second sense, not the first. For him, a *lure* is an inwardly felt goal toward which a person feels drawn; an attractive possibility that one wants to actualize. When a fish swims toward a worm, the worm functions as lure for the fish; and when a person feels beckoned toward the ideal of a just society, that ideal likewise functions as a lure. Thus a lure is experienced as a goal, an object of desire. A *lure for feeling* is an attractive possibility that pertains to the subjective dimension of human life: to how one might feel on the inside psychologically and to how one might feel the presence of the surrounding world, including other people. Propositions, then, are means by which cultures can be transformed and also means by which cultures are sustained, whether healthy or unhealthy. Propositions can be transmitted by a wide variety of means, only some of which are verbal. In the culture of consumerism, advertisements are an essential means by which propositions or "lures for feeling" are conveyed to the general population. The propositions often pertain to prospects for conspicuous consumption, and they are transmitted not simply through words but through music and images. When people in a shopping mall see a model dressed in fashionable clothing, the model functions as a lure for feeling. Of course, advertisements are but one means by which propositions are transmitted. More generally they seem to be transmitted in at least three ways: through humanly created artifacts, through the natural world, and through other people.

When transmitted by artifacts, propositions are prompted by images and sounds from the humanly built environment that have been created by human beings from materials supplied by the Earth. This means that cities can be designed and buildings constructed in ways that enable people to feel certain moods and enjoy certain kinds of relations with one another. Anyone entering a Buddhist temple in China understands this. The temple conveys a mood. And of course the same applies to buildings, streets, sidewalks, and interior design. This is why urban design is so important. How a city is constructed can affect how people feel about themselves and others. The creative and performing arts, too, are among the most influential means by which lures for feeling are transmitted. A Chinese landscape painting, with its images of rivers and mountains without end, and with human communities situated in terms of a larger and more dynamic whole, conveys a certain way to live in the world: namely that of harmony with nature. When it comes to lures for feeling, there are many material expressions.

The natural world, too, can be a source of propositions and, thus, of human culture. In China, one of the geniuses of Taoism is that it has invited the Chinese to allow themselves not simply to mold the natural world for human purposes, but also to fit into the natural world, allowing its own energies and beauty to shape human consciousness. In effect, the natural world has been a source of meanings, of propositions, of lures for feeling. The sensuous resonances of real rivers and real mountains have been sources for culture. In the United States the writings of Thoreau and Ralph Waldo Emerson, and of contemporary filmmakers who document the wonders of animals and landscapes, point in a similar direction.

But people—and more specifically role models—are also means by which "lures for feeling" get transmitted. The propositions—that is, the relevant ideals—are transmitted not only by what people say, but also, and perhaps more deeply, by what they do and feel. Lures for feeling can also be transmitted from one person to another and reinforced by means of more direct perceptions. They can be caught, as it were, in a process of psychological osmosis, not unlike the way in which people catch diseases. When we catch diseases from other people, we are infected by the germs in their bodies without our even knowing it, such that their physical chemistry becomes our own. In a similar way, we can catch the attitudes and values of others and become shaped by them, so that their mental chemistry becomes part of our own.

In a consumer society, celebrities play a dominant role in all of this. With the role of media in human life, people want to be like and live like celebrities and movie stars: the ones who are photogenic and seem happy all the time. Teenagers and adults alike seek to internalize their moods, desires, and attitudes. Thus a great amount of "education" occurs in this way in a consumer-driven society. It occurs through advertisements and popular culture. We might call this informal education, thus distinguishing it from the more formal education that occurs in the classroom.

One challenge of formal education today, then, is to help young people discover worthwhile values that transcend the limitations of market-driven values and the shallowness of popular culture. This is not to say that popular culture is always shallow. Sometimes the music of Radiohead and U2 can be quite profound and can indeed be an ally in cultural transformation toward healthy ends. In any case, the need is for education to be a context in which students grow in their capacities for wisdom, compassion, and creativity, and not simply in their capacities for memorizing facts, passing tests, and acquiring skills that enable them to find jobs and help contribute to a growing economy. The need is for moral education and aesthetic education.

In a Whiteheadian context, moral and aesthetic education cannot be sharply separated. This is because both deal with creative harmony. Moral education helps people live in creative harmony with other people, respecting others as ends in themselves and not simply means to other ends. It can also help people live in creative harmony with the natural world, enabling them to realize that they are small, but included in the larger whole of the web of life. Thus moral education has as its aims social justice, understood as respect and care for persons, and also ecological sustainability, understood as respect and care for the larger community of life.

Aesthetic education helps people discover higher ideals by which to live, as discovered in the arts and sciences. There is, or can be, an aesthetic dimension to science education as well as to education in the arts. People can enjoy the beauty of mathematical equations and the adventures of scientific discovery, even as they enjoy the beauty of music and painting and literature. The Whiteheadian point of view emphasizes that science and art can both be contexts in which people discover higher ideals by which to live. Science and mathematics may not offer values by which to live, but both can give a sense for the mystery and beauty of the universe itself. The need in formal education is to arrive at modes of pedagogy in science and the arts that make them as interesting in their ways, as is popular culture in its way. As formal education explores new forms of pedagogy that enliven the minds and hearts of students, it becomes a means to the end of cultural transformation.

PERSUASION NOT COERCION

Cultural transformations can be healthy or unhealthy. The evolution of society into a culture of greed is a transformation of sorts, but from the point of view of process thinkers it is not a healthy transformation. A healthy transformation will be one in which people are inspired to share in one another's destinies in ways where all enjoy healthy consumption, with no one left behind.

In principle, transformations of both kinds—the healthy and unhealthy—can be elicited in many ways. Sometimes they are produced by national disasters and catastrophes, in which people learn to share in each other's destinies out of need and, perhaps, facing a common enemy. This is how war works. We see people sharing in the destinies of others because they have developed animosity toward an "other" who is depicted as demonic. Cultural transformations can also occur by force when an authority from above seeks to effect the transformation from the top down. This is what sometimes happens in authoritarian forms of religion and in misguided governmental attempts to dramatically alter a society.

But cultural transformation can also occur from the bottom up, in a grassroots way, as people begin to share a common hope that life can be different, and as they see meaningful examples of this different way of living. This is a more Confucian and Whiteheadian approach. It teaches by inspiration and example rather than by coercion. As Whiteheadians discuss the emergence of a constructively postmodern culture, they have this latter path in mind. They believe that the most meaningful changes in life come about from the inside out, when people are persuaded that there is a better and more hopeful way to live, and they are inspired by others who show the way.

Part of process thought emphasizes the importance of persuasion over coercion. In process thought, even the divine reality—even

God—acts through persuasion rather than coercion, invitation rather than force. People do not meet God by hearing others preach of God; they meet God when they encounter others who love them and care for them. They see God in the gentle actions of others who inspire them. If God can operate in this gentle way, then we can do so as well. The aim is not to force constructive postmodernism on people but to propose it as a better way to live, letting people decide for themselves.

Formal education can be one place where students learn to "decide for themselves." Their teachers can adopt what might be called a proposative model of education. A proposative model differs from an authoritarian model in that it proposes ideas for consideration, rather than imposing them. It understands the educational process itself as including a dialogical component, whereby the teacher shares wisdom and ideas that come from years of experience, but where the teacher's aim is also to help students respond to those ideas in ways that can include criticism of the ideas themselves. Thus, the classroom becomes a context for free, non-coercive discussion. In a society dominated by so much media and so much authority, the very act of having a free space—a space where people can seek truth together, without presuming that all must agree—is itself a radical act. It creates space, among other things, for cultural transformation to occur from the inside out, and from the ground up.

Appendix C:
The Many Become One
and Are Increased by One

WE HAVE SEEN that Whitehead envisions the universe as a dynamic and evolving whole in which every event is related to every other event. He makes the further claim that each event is a gathering of some aspect of the universe into itself. The British poet William Blake begins his poem, "Auguries of Innocence," by inviting his readers to learn to see the world in a grain of sand and heaven in a wildflower and eternity in an hour. Whitehead invites his readers to see the universe in each present moment.

Imagine a mountain above the Columbia River. For Whitehead, a momentary energy-event within the depths of an atom within this mountain would be an example of an event; and so would a moment of experience in the life of a woman who is taking a ride in a boat, gazing at the mountain from a distance and enjoying its shapes. In the foreground of her visual awareness she sees the mountain, and in the background she sees the river and a fisherman on it. From Whitehead's point of view both of these activities—the energy-event in the depths of the atom and the experience in the life of the woman—exhibit a similar structure. They are acts in which the many become one and are increased by one. This saying—"the many become one and are increased by one"—gets at the very heart of Whitehead's vision of reality (PR 21).

To illustrate its meaning, let us consider the woman. As she gazes at the mountain, she sees at least three things: the mountain, the river, and the fisherman. These three items—the mountain and the river and the boat—will be together in her act of experiencing them. This is what Whitehead means by becoming one. He means that in experiencing things, the things we experience are gathered into the subjective unity—that is, the subjective harmony—of a single experience. In *Adventures of Ideas* he puts the point this way: "No things are 'together' except as together in experience" (AI 236). Experience is in the world, and the world is in experience.

When Whitehead says that the many are then increased by one, he means that, as soon as the experience of unifying the world occurs, the experience then becomes an additional object in the history of the universe, albeit one that resides within her memory. The experience becomes objectively immortal, in that it becomes part of the ongoing history of the universe. Of course the woman may never think about the experience again, at least in a conscious way. Even if the woman forgets the experience of looking at the mountain at a conscious level, the experience is part of her life at an unconscious level. If, by chance, she travels again to this place and looks at the same mountain a second time, something new will have been added: namely, her original act of seeing the mountain. Thus her life is an ongoing process amid which, at every moment, the many become one and are increased by one. In Whitehead's words: "The ancient doctrine that 'no one crosses the same river twice' is extended. No thinker thinks twice; and, to put the matter more generally, no subject experiences twice" (PR 29).

From Whitehead's point of view, an electron in the depths of an atom exhibits the same dynamic. No electron experiences twice either. The electron may seem to be a particle that travels through space, but in fact, thinks Whitehead, it is a series of momentary energy-events, each of which inherits from the past, not unlike the way in which the woman's life is an ongoing series of momentary experiences, each of which inherits from its past. An analogy might be frames in a movie. The movie unfolds in a continuous way, from one frame to another, but the reality of the situation is that the movie is composed of the momentary frames. It is the momentary frames that create the sense of continuity. The life of an electron and that of a human being unfold in a similar way: moment by moment. "There is a becoming of continuity," says Whitehead, "but no continuity of becoming" (PR 53).

Of course, electrons do not "live" in the same way that humans live. They are not conscious or reflective; they do not have hopes for building a just society. Still, electrons have worlds to which they are responsive. As Whitehead sees it, each momentary burst of energy—each quantum event—gathers its own submicroscopic world into unity for a moment, and then the immediacy of that act of gathering perishes, such that the moment becomes objectively immortal in what comes afterward. Here, too, "the many become one and are increased by one."

In this act of gathering that submicroscopic world into unity, the energy-event is influenced or causally affected by what is gathered into unity. It is shaped and determined by its submicroscopic world. This is what we mean by causation. Whitehead means that as an event occurs, it is inevitably shaped and partly caused by what affects it. And yet he also believes that nothing in the universe is completely determined. In the act of receiving those influences, the energy-event has a spark of creativity, on the basis of which it actualizes certain possibilities for receiving the influences and thus cuts off other possibilities. In this way, it exhibits a kind of quantum indeterminacy. The basic thesis of Whitehead is that the energy-events within matter are early, evolutionary examples of what, later in the history of the cosmos, we call actual occasions of experience in the lives of human beings and other animals. There is an ontological continuity between energy at the level of inorganic realities and subjective experience at the level of living beings. Descartes divided the world into two kinds of substances: material objects and immaterial minds. Whitehead proposes that there is one kind actuality: moments or drops of experience.

This means that in every moment of human experience some feature of the universe is gathered into the unity of the single act. In being gathered into this unity, many things in the external world become part of the one thing that is occurring in the moment. For Whitehead, this was one of the most important aspects of his philosophy; namely, the idea that two entities can be present in one another. He puts it this way in *Process and Reality:*

> The principle of universal relativity directly traverses Aristotle's dictum, "A substance is not present in a subject." On the contrary, according to this principle, an actual entity is present in other actual entities. In fact if we allow for degrees of relevance, and for negligible relevance, we must say that every actual entity is present in every other actual entity. The philosophy of organism is mainly devoted to the task of making clear the notion of being present in another entity. (50)

Elsewhere Whitehead speaks of each moment of human experience, and for that matter each energy-event within the depths of matter, as "a concrescence of the universe" (PR 51).

Appendix D:
The Principle of
Universal Relativity

IN THE EXCERPT from Whitehead quoted in Appendix C, he uses the phrase "the principle of universal relativity." This is the idea that every moment of experience includes an aspect of every entity in the universe. Of course, this idea is very Buddhist in tone. A powerful example of this way of thinking is found in the tradition of *Hua Yen* Buddhism, which compares the entire universe to a vast network of jewels in which each entity mirrors every other entity. If you put a dot on one of the jewels, that dot would then be mirrored in every other. Whitehead believed that modern physics points in the same direction. In *Science and the Modern World,* he writes:

> In a certain sense, everything is everywhere at all times. For every location involves an aspect of itself in every other location. Thus every spatio-temporal standpoint mirrors the world. (114)

For many process thinkers, then, the most important idea in Whitehead is not simply that all things are in process; it is that all things are interconnected or interrelated. It is that, in a certain sense, everything is everywhere at all times.

The idea that everything is everywhere does not mean that "things" are not "things." In Whitehead's philosophy, mountains remain mountains, plants remain plants, and people remain people. Whiteheadian process thinkers further emphasize that the connections are internal relations rather than external relations. An external relation is a relation between two things that does not really affect the identity or existence of the thing at issue. For example, if two boxes are placed on a table and then one of them is moved, the spatial relation changes, but the boxes seem to remain the same. They seem to be externally related to one another. An internal relation is a relation between two things where the relations partly determine the identity and existence of at least one of the things at issue. For example, if two people are sitting at the table and talking and listening to each other, their words and voices are partly determining the states of consciousness in the other. From a Whiteheadian perspective, their states of consciousness are not separable from their existence at that moment, because their existence is their experience in the moment. Their relation is an intersubjective relation. They would not be who they are at that moment without the other person.

For Whitehead, the whole of the universe is akin to a vast web of intersubjective relations, in which the energies of the Ten Thousand Things are shared with one another even as the items remain distinct. Relationality does not simply mean that individuals are parts of greater wholes; it also means that wholes are ingredient in each part. To repeat: each actual entity is a concrescence of the universe.

Appendix E:
Beauty and the Beautiful

O F COURSE, most of us do not experience something as grand as "the universe" in the comings and goings of our daily lives. We may look up at the stars and get a sense of a greater whole, but most often we are looking across the street or into the faces of people we encounter in the workplace, or at the food on our table. We meet the universe most concretely in the immediacy of local settings: in our homes, our workplace, our villages and cities, our natural landscapes; and in our friends and family members and the strangers we pass on the street. We cannot live our lives in perpetual mystical amazement at the oneness of it all. We must eat and drink and work and sleep.

Thus the question emerges: What difference does it really make that all things are interconnected? For most process thinkers, it makes all the difference in the world. It means that our task in life is to live in creative harmony with people and other living beings in these local settings, adding our own distinctive kinds of beauty to the larger whole. This beauty can be communal as well as individual; it can be a way in which people live together with one another, in ways that are socially just, ecologically sustainable, and spiritually satisfying, with no one left behind.

Here beauty does not refer to how things appear on the outside, but to who we are on the inside. In *Adventures of Ideas,* Whitehead draws a distinction between the beautiful, which is a property of objects perceived; and beauty, which is quality of subjective immediacy and emotional well-being that can occur in perceiving those objects (AI 225). To be sure, the two go together. People's capacities to live in beauty with one another are influenced by their built and natural environments. If a person's environment includes unclean water and denuded topsoil such that there is no food to eat, it is not easy to have a sense of emotional well-being. This is one reason why poverty is tragic. And this is why a life of creative harmony must include compassion for others, sharing in their destinies, and working to build just and sustainable communities. The principle of relativity says that we share in one another's destinies even if we do not realize it.

A just society, then, is simultaneously a beautiful society; that is, a society in which the natural and built environments are conducive to healthy living for all. And a beautiful society is one in which people can live with satisfaction, enjoying different kinds of beauty. In process thought, there are many kinds of beauty: love and courage, wisdom and compassion, creativity and laughter, faith and hope, struggle and peace. All are forms of harmony and intensity.

Whiteheadian thought then adds that even as we add our own beauty to the larger whole, we can be enriched by the beauty of others: the hills and rivers, the plants and animals, and trees and stars. Human experience is not only active; it is also receptive. We receive others into our lives through experience in the mode of causal efficacy, and the enjoyment of their presence is one of the gifts of life. Thus the value of our lives is not simply what we make of our lives. It is also what we receive into our lives. In process thought, value is not simply a human projection onto a blank slate. It is something that is found in other people and also throughout the natural world.

Thus, Whitehead seeks to overcome the separation of fact and value that is so common in modern thinking. Often, in the modern world, we assume that "facts" are part of objective reality and that "values" are projections onto that reality. Certainly, there is truth in this. Sometimes humans do indeed impute values to things that do not deserve them. We elevate celebrities into the status of gods when they are just people. We elevate certain cultures over others when the cultures are of equal value.

Nevertheless, Whitehead believes that there is also a certain kind of value in the world even apart from human projections; namely, the value that other living beings have in and for themselves as they struggle to survive with satisfaction. For example, when an animal struggles to find food, the animal experiences "survival" as a value, and the acquisition of food is itself a realization of value, at least for the animal. The Whiteheadian view is that this kind of value was part of the Earth long before humans evolved, and thus there are values in nature even if humans do not recognize them. Part of living in creative harmony with the wider world is to recognize this value in nature and, of course, the value of other people, as well. It is to treat other persons as ends in themselves and not simply as means to other ends.

In short, the principle of relativity has numerous implications for human life. This means that individual human beings have their existence and identity in relation to the communities in which they are nested, both human and ecological. We are persons-in-community rather than persons-in-isolation. It means that our emotions and ideas, even as they might seem to lie inside us, are not simply isolated conditions lying within our bodies and minds. They are ways of being related to others. It means that the environments we can and should build are cities and villages that are conducive to living in creative harmony with others. And it means that, as we do so, we add beauty to the larger whole of the Earth and to the universe.

Appendix F:
Practical Guidelines for
Decision-Making
(The Earth Charter)

1. Respect Earth and life in all its diversity.

2. Care for the community of life with understanding, compassion, and love.

3. Build democratic societies that are just, participatory, sustainable, and peaceful.

4. Secure Earth's bounty and beauty for present and future generations.

5. Protect and restore the integrity of Earth's ecological systems, with special concern for biological diversity and the natural processes that sustain life.

6. Prevent harm as the best method of environmental protection and, when knowledge is limited, apply a precautionary approach.

7. Adopt patterns of production, consumption, and reproduction that safeguard Earth's regenerative capacities, human rights, and community well-being.

8. Advance the study of ecological sustainability and promote the open exchange and wide application of the knowledge acquired.

9. Eradicate poverty as an ethical, social, and environmental imperative.

10. Ensure that economic activities and institutions at all levels promote human development in an equitable and sustainable manner.

11. Affirm gender equality and equity as prerequisites to sustainable development and ensure universal access to education, health care, and economic opportunity.

12. Uphold the right of all, without discrimination, to a natural and social environment supportive of human dignity, bodily health, and spiritual well-being, with special attention to the rights of indigenous peoples and minorities.

13. Strengthen democratic institutions at all levels, and provide transparency and accountability in governance, inclusive participation in decision making, and access to justice.

14. Integrate into formal education and life-long learning the knowledge, values, and skills needed for a sustainable way of life.

15. Treat all living beings with respect and consideration.

16. Promote a culture of tolerance, nonviolence, and peace.

For the complete Earth Charter, including the preamble and supportive points, see: www.earthcharter.org.

Epilogue:
What Is Process Theology?

SOMETIMES PEOPLE CONFUSE *process thought* with Christian process theology. This is a problem. *Process thought* is an intellectual and cultural movement influenced by the philosophy of Whitehead. It is international in scope, with advocates on every continent, and who come from many walks of life. Some are philosophers, but others are schoolteachers, economists, environmentalists, mathematicians, business leaders, musicians, and poets. Some are Christian, some Jewish, some Buddhist, some Hindu, some Marxist, and some have no religion at all. They form part of a community of people who are influenced in varying degrees and ways by Whitehead. They are the international Whitehead community.

What do they hold in common? They all think that everything is interconnected, that all things are in process, that each living being has intrinsic value, and that the best future for the world is to build communities that are creative, compassionate, participatory, equitable, ecologically wise, and spiritually satisfying with no one left behind. They realize that many other people also hold these ideas and values. They do not think that the whole world needs to convert to Whiteheadianism. But they do think that Whitehead offers unique and powerful support for these ideas and values.

Who, then, are Christians influenced by Whitehead's thought? At one level they are merely a subcommunity within the larger Whiteheadian community. Nevertheless, members of this sub-community have been some of the most influential within the overall process movement. The role of Christian process theology in the process movement is good news to people who are interested in religion, but problematic for people who are eager to see process thought speak to a wide variety of people, some of whom may not be interested in religion at all. One of the reasons I have written this book is to introduce process thought to people who are interested in learning about it, even if they have no interest in religion. The idea for the book emerged in my own mind while teaching courses in process thought in China, where sometimes it seemed relevant to mention "religion," but sometimes not.

Still, the whole tradition of process thought is deeply indebted to the pioneering work of Christian process theologians, especially to John B. Cobb, Jr., whose own work has kept so much of the Whiteheadian tradition alive. An introduction to process thought would be incomplete without a brief introduction to process theology. By way of an epilogue, then, I address one more question: *What is process theology?*

The question is difficult to address, because process theology is itself in process. I have said that process *thought* is like a novel in the making, with new generations adding new chapters. So it is with process *theology*. Today process theologians in the Christian tradition are developing mystical theologies, political theologies, feminist theologies, biblical theologies, postcolonial theologies, evangelical theologies, and post-Western theologies. In the future, I predict that they will be developing Pentecostal process theologies. On the one hand, the variety can be bewildering, especially to outsiders. But on the other, it is precisely what draws people to Christian process theology in the first place. Process theology is an inclusive tradition that welcomes a variety of voices and perspectives and that cannot be reduced to one voice.

Process theology is also a multireligious tradition. For the sake of brevity I am using the phrase "process theology" as an abbreviation for *Christian* process theology. But I do so with great reluctance. If "theology" names a religiously inspired way of thinking, then today there are other important kinds of process theology: Jewish, Buddhist, Muslim, and Hindu, for example. Additionally, in East Asia, there are many who are interpreting Confucianism and Taoism with help from Whitehead, sometimes considering these traditions as "religions" and sometimes as "cultural traditions."

Just as process thought is not reducible to process theology, so process theology is not reducible to Christian process theology. This is good news for all process theologians, including the Christians. There can be no peace in the world unless there is peace among religions. With the emergence of process theology as a multireligious subcommunity, it becomes possible that Whitehead's philosophy might provide a conceptual vocabulary by which people from many different religious traditions might interpret themselves to one another, learn from each other, and work together to build sustainable, multireligious communities. It is within the context of a multireligious world, and also a multireligious process tradition, that we consider Christian process theology.

PROCESS THEOLOGY IN PROCESS

Christian process theology—from here on, "process theology"—emerged in the 1950s in the United States, and, for most of its history, it has been developed by Western Christian theologians in the United States and, to some degree, in Europe. Many among the first generations of process theologians were primarily preoccupied with metaphysical considerations. In particular they were concerned with ways that Whitehead's understanding of God could help reconcile science and religion, science and philosophy, and, more poignantly, how it could reconcile God with evil.

Here, a word about "evil" is in order. Evil is understood in different ways by different process thinkers. For my part, I think of it as tragedy: that is, (1) the debilitating suffering from which humans and other living beings suffer, and which, all things considered, would have been better had things been otherwise; and also (2) the missed potential from which many also suffer, as occurs when a young child suffers from cancer. Some of this tragedy is caused by human beings, and some is not. Many in the first generation of process theologians in the Christian tradition turned to process theology because it presented a plausible way of understanding how an all-loving God does not cause such tragedy, and cannot prevent it, but nevertheless shares in the suffering and provides hope amid its devastating effects. As Christians they saw this God as the very kind of God revealed in Jesus. If Jesus is a window to the divine, they said, Jesus reveals the humanity and vulnerability of God.

Today, however, a new generation of process-oriented thinkers is emerging, and their interests in process theology cover a much wider range. They are still interested in God and science, God and philosophy, and God and suffering. Additionally they are deeply absorbed in many subjects besides God, however named, and they grow weary—even bored—with thinking that theology must always be about God. I am reminded of an incident many years ago when I taught an entire course called Contemporary Ideas of God to college undergraduates. I was proud of myself because I had developed a scheme with sixteen ways of thinking about God, the last of which was the process approach. I drew diagrams on the board for each view, and was quite sure that the students would love the course. At the end of the course one student, a favorite of mine, came up to me afterwards and said: "Thank you for this course; I learned a lot from it." I asked her what she learned, and she said: "I learned that I am not interested in God." She then added: "I am more interested in a spirituality of connectedness than a spirituality of God."

Immediately, I knew what she meant. She meant that she found the sacred, however named, in felt and mutually enhancing relations with other people and the natural world, not with a transcendent entity which, to her, seemed like a focal point in the male imagination. Her notion of a spirituality of connectedness gave me new eyes for many religious traditions, including Confucianism, in which notions of a transcendent deity seem less important than notions of relationship. I coined the phrase the "horizontal sacred" to name this other way of experiencing the sacred. My point here, then, is that first-generation process theologians were interested in the "vertical sacred," but that the new generation is at least as interested in the horizontal sacred, and in very practical ways. They are interested in Christian approaches to the environment, inter-religious dialogue, sustainability, counseling, gender relations, race, politics, literature, music, economics, healthcare, and spirituality. If a parliament of process theologians occurred, and participants were asked why they are drawn to process theology, they might focus on its relevance to the life of discipleship.

THE LIFE OF DISCIPLESHIP

Among process theologians, there are two complementary ways of understanding Christianity: one objective and descriptive, and one more theological and normative. From the first perspective, Christianity is a multigenerational, social, and historical movement, with many different expressions, that began sometime after the death of Jesus and has been evolving ever since in many different directions. Process theologians who understand Christianity in this way emphasize that it is a tradition in process, and that new generations of Christians can add to its history. They add that responsible participation in the tradition lies in demonstrating meaningful continuity with the past, building upon inherited resources that elicit wisdom and compassion, but also acknowledging the failings of the past: its patriarchy, its neglect of the Earth and nonhuman animals, its arrogance toward other religions, its imperialism, its insensitivity to diverse sexual orientations, and its tendencies toward violence. Another name for the latter acknowledgment is repentance. For process theologians as for biblical theologians, repentance does not necessarily involve a sense of guilt, but it does require a desire to turn around from the sins of the past and move constructively into the future. Process theologians believe that Christians can repent as individuals and as a community.

The second way of understanding Christianity is more theological and normative. It seeks to understand Christianity not as it has been in the past, or even as it is in the present, but rather as it should be and ought to be, if it is faithful to the healing ministry of Jesus and the wisdom of tradition. Of course no given Christian can stand outside his or her social location and declare with perfect objectivity what this "ideal Christianity" might look like. But many process theologians have developed various versions of the ideal, and in what follows I will present the outline of a view often found.

As the first Christians came into existence, they were not called Christians. They were called people of the Way. Process theologians appreciate this terminology, because they believe that Christianity—and for that matter every religion—is a way of living. A way of living cannot be reduced to a way of thinking or a way of feeling or a way of acting. It is not simply a worldview or an application of a worldview. It is an orientation toward life guided by a set of subjective aims. It involves the whole of one's life:

head, hands, and heart. According to this way of thinking, there is no sharp dichotomy between religion and culture. In China, for example, Confucianism and Taoism are often considered cultural traditions but not religions. From a process perspective there is no need to quibble over the word "religion." They are ways of living.

What, then, would be the guiding aim of the Christian way of living? Process theologians would agree with most other Christians. It is to be faithful to God as God was revealed in Christ. Here, the word faith means more than belief, at least if "belief" is understood as intellectual assent to ideas. Faith means trust in God. Imagine someone learning to float in the shallow waters of a sea. The person may assent to the idea that the sea can support her, but she may still try to grasp the water and sink. In order to be supported by the sea, she must somehow cease trying to grab the water and allow her own fears to drop away. She must trust the water. For process theologians, as for most Christians, this trust can be facilitated by belief in God, but it can also be obstructed by an overly fervent belief that evokes excessive clinging. If we trust God, says the process theologian, we best realize that God cannot be grasped as an object among objects in physical or mental space, and that God can flow within our lives only if we realize, among other things, that God is always more than our concept of God. Thus trust in God requires a healthy sense of mystery.

Still the question remains: What does it mean to trust God *as revealed in Christ?* It lies in sharing in the journey of Christ and extending that journey. This sharing does not require repeating every belief of Jesus or imitating his every action. It does not even require believing that Jesus was totally devoid of sin. There may well have been times in Jesus' life when he became angry when he should have been more tender, thus missing the mark of responding to God's lure for his life. But it does involve trying to be open to God in one's own way and time, as Jesus was in his way and his time. This involves a willingness to be creatively transformed, again and again, by the face of the stranger, the beauty of nature, the changing circumstances of life, and the ever-adaptive callings of God. For process theologians this is what it means to *live in Christ* or to *walk with Christ* or to *follow Christ*.

CHRIST AS LOGOS

For process theologians such as John B. Cobb, Jr., the *Christ* who is followed is not reducible to the historical Jesus but is also the calling presence of God, dwelling inside the human heart and also within the rest of nature, the one who beckons toward creative transformation. The Gospel of John speaks of this beckoning presence as the divine Logos and says that it was revealed but not exhausted in the healing ministry of Jesus. Let us speak of it simply as the Spirit of God at work in the world. On this view, the Christian is one who seeks, with Jesus, to live from this Spirit.

The New Testament says that a person who lives from this Spirit has "put on the mind of Christ." If a person puts on this mind, she is open to the sacrament of each present moment and also to the past and future. On the one hand, her mind can be inspired by the stories of Jesus as recounted in the New Testament and by the liturgies of the church. She is nourished by what process theologians call the causal efficacy of the past. But her face must also be turned toward the future and thus receptive to fresh promptings from the Spirit. She must be open to novel possibilities, derived from God, which have no exact parallel in the Christian past but which, if actualized, bring hope to the world. Thus a walk with Christ is not a mechanical process derived from already existing rules for walking but rather a creative and flexible process, in which one's footsteps help create the path.

Most Christians who are influenced by process theology find that a walk with Christ is both freeing and challenging. It is freeing because it involves being open to the freshness of the divine Spirit, which can both animate and empower a person, day by day and moment by moment. One who walks with Christ is free to enjoy the sacrament of each present moment. From a process perspective, the Christian life involves a healthy balance of work, prayer, and relaxation, in all of which God can be present. Nevertheless, a walk with Christ is also difficult because it involves living from a set of values that are not often supported by the surrounding world. In the twenty-first century, the surrounding world for many people is the culture of consumerism. This culture tells us that we are saved or made whole by appearance, affluence, and marketable achievement. A walk with Christ approaches life with a very different set of values. It sees wisdom and compassion as much more important than appearance and affluence; it sees the face of God in the poor and powerless; it struggles against the principalities and powers of injustice; it prizes nonviolence over violence; it rejects revenge; it values humility over celebrity; it risks having faith in God's love even when that love seems absent; and it seeks to live simply in the world, without too many possessions, so that others can simply live.

Of course few Christians undertake this walk consistently and completely. Many fall short of it. But this way of living—this kind of walking—is the life of discipleship to which Christianity points. The Christian trusts that God is in the walking itself and not simply in the destination, and that God also provides the power to begin anew when the walker falls short of the walking. A Zen master was once asked what is it like to be enlightened, and he responded: "When I fall down, I get up again." Process theologians appreciate the spirit of his response and add that God's Spirit is found in the energy to get up again.

PANENTHEISM

Thus the question emerges: What is God in process theology? Process theologians understand God as encompassing Life, within whom the universe unfolds. This way of thinking about God is sometimes called panentheism: a word which literally means everything-in-God. Panentheism is different from pantheism. Pantheism is the view that the totality of finite actualities is identical with God. Panentheism, by contrast, is the view that all actualities are somehow part of God, but also that God is more than everything added together.

In the Whiteheadian version of panentheism, as developed in *Process and Reality,* God has three aspects. God is (1) a nontemporal mind who envisions all the potentialities which the many beings in the universe can actualize; (2) an everlasting consciousness filled with compassion who empathically receives the world into the divine life, moment by moment, and (3) a guiding presence in the universe who dwells within the depths of each creature, luring it to exercise its creativity in creating the best possible outcome for the situation at hand. The first aspect is called the Primordial Nature of God. The second is called the Consequent Nature. And the third is generally understood as the way in which the Primordial Nature is in the world.

Some, but not all, process theologians are Trinitarian in perspective, and the three aspects of God just named can suggest something like a doctrine of the Trinity. The Mind of the universe, understood as a holding tank or reservoir of timeless possibilities, would be similar to "God the Creator." The Compassion would be the side of God revealed but not exhausted in Jesus. And the guiding presence would be the Spirit of God.

For many process theologians, what is most important about the doctrine of the Trinity is not that it illuminates the interior life of God, which will forever be a mystery, but rather that, in a more general way, it points to the primacy of relationality in understanding human life. If we humans are made in the image of God, and if God is in some way Trinitarian, then humans are made in the image of the Trinity. This means that we rightly find our own well-being in community with other people and the natural world, just as God finds God's own well-being in felt relations with the world. There can be no isolated salvation. We are saved together or not saved at all.

Process theology proposes that God finds God's own well-being in felt relations with the world. The everlasting consciousness of God—the Consequent Nature—is itself a receptacle for the experiences of all that happens in the universe and is inwardly composed of those happenings. This leads some process theologians to speak of the universe as the body of God. The universe is not the body of God in the sense that everything that happens in the universe is a result of divine agency, but rather in the sense that God feels the happenings of the universe much like we feel the happenings in our own bodies; that is, as inside us yet more than us.

How can this be understood? Perhaps one way to understand how the universe is inside God is to compare the universe to an embryo within the womb of a mother. The analogy is apt in three ways. First, the embryo has its own life, which means that things can happen in its unfolding that cannot be controlled by the mother. Similarly, say process theologians, things can and do happen in the universe, by virtue of the creativity of the universe itself, which cannot be controlled by God. This is how process theologians explain the tragedies of our world, both natural and humanly made. Cancer and murder, tsunamis and rapes, are not the product of divine agency, but the result of the power and creativity of the world itself. This creativity, already introduced in the core of this essay, is neither good nor evil in itself but can unfold in many different ways, some tragic and some beautiful. God is an instance of this creativity, but not the only instance. All creatures in the world—including cancer cells and murderers—embody it, too.

Nevertheless, and second, what happens in the embryo is felt by the mother and is part of her. Similarly, say process theologians, what happens to each entity in the universe—to every human being—is felt by God and affects God. This is how process theology begins to talk about prayers in which a person addresses God as a Thou and not an It. When humans address God, they often sense that their prayers are being received into a deeper listening as the prayer occurs, and that the listener who listens is affected by the prayer. Process theologians agree. The Consequent Nature of God is the deep listening. For many people, of course, the question is how God answers prayers. For process theologians, God does not and cannot answer prayers by manipulating situations in a unilateral way; but the very act of praying can alter the situation of the one praying and also the ones prayed for, such that God is better able to act in their lives. It is important to emphasize, though, that petitionary prayer is but one kind of prayer. Prayer understood in this way is one instance of the more general idea that all the experiences of all living beings—whether happy or sad, constructive or destructive—affect God and become part of God as they occur. No one suffers alone.

Third, the analogy of the universe within the womb of a mother rightly suggests that God is active in the world in a noncoercive but perpetually influential way. In the case of a mother in pregnancy, this activity takes the form of amniotic fluid that nourishes the developing embryo and perhaps also influences the attitude of the mother. In the case of God, this activity takes the form of "initial aims," which represent the way in which God is immanent in the universe, even as the universe is also immanent within God. I will explain initial aims shortly, but first a further word is in order about alternative images of God, such as that of Mother.

Needless to say this image of God as Mother and the universe as a womb can be controversial to at least two sets of people: very traditional Christians for whom male imagery of God is the only relevant imagery, and feminist Christians who want to avoid stereotyping women as finding their fulfillment in, and only in, pregnancy. The good news among process-oriented Christians is that there are many feminist Christians who help critique these stereotypes and who offer alternative images. But the image of God as Mother is indeed challenging to more traditional Christians, and this challenge, on the part of process theologians, is in some ways very intentional.

BEYOND GOD THE POTTER

Process theologians employ such images in order to provide a constructive alternative to an image of God that too often dominates the monotheistic imagination. We might call it (1) the *externalist* perspective, because it imagines God as completely external to the world; or (2) the *unilateralist* perspective, because it sees God's power as one-sided or unilateral and thus capable of molding the world according to divine will; or simply (3) the patriarchal perspective, because it imagines God on the analogy of a powerful male ruler who wields power but is not empathic. On this view, the relation of God to the world is analogous to that of a Potter and the pot that "he" is molding. The Potter is external to the pot, and the pot's destiny is largely determined by the will and power of the Potter. Process theologians reject this image of God the Potter. They think God is more loving, and that the ministry of Jesus is one place where this love can be seen.

For many Christians, the image of a parent and child is much more relevant than that of a potter and pot. This is the beauty of envisioning God as Father or Mother. Process theologians understand and appreciate this preference for parental imagery, but then add that, in an authentic Christian life, there is no need for Christians to always understand themselves as children in God's presence. It is all right to be an adult in God's presence, too, and thus to add one's own voice to the ongoing life of God. This is the wisdom of the Psalms, where so often the Psalmist laments or protests, sometimes against God. For process theologians there is something right about this approach to God. It allows human beings to share with God the whole of their lives and to own their own feelings.

Still, it remains the case that, for process theologians, the ultimate nature of God is love. From a process perspective, love has two sides: (1) an empathic side, which listens to others and is affected and changed by what is heard and felt and (2) an active side, which responds to what is listened to by providing possibilities for well-being. Jesus showed these two sides of love in countless ways: by listening to others and sharing in their suffering; by taking delight in the faith of others and the innocence of children; by comforting the afflicted, especially those who were despised by others; and by afflicting the comfortable, especially those who thought they were better than others. At the end of his life, he also revealed a nonviolent side of love by dying on a cross rather than responding to violence with violence. In these various activities, Jesus showed that a life of love is flexible and improvisational. It does not follow a perfectly scripted blueprint, because it realizes that each new situation requires a slightly different response. In seeking to walk in love, Jesus seems to have realized that each moment has its calling.

In process theology, the callings of the moment are called the "initial aims." These initial aims are the callings of the moment to which Jesus was responsive in his way. They differ from moment to moment, but always they are for the well-being of life relative to the situation at hand. The phrase "initial aims" is not especially melodious, but it does use a word that is very important to process theologians. The word "initial" is meant to suggest that God's callings are present in the beginning of each moment of experience at an unconscious but powerful level. Initial aims consist of possibilities that people can actualize, and they also contain within them the felt hope that they will be actualized.

For process theologians, this felt hope belongs both to God and to the person. Thus the aims of God within human life are

God's hopes for the person, but also the person's hope for himself or herself. These aims are for the well-being of life, but the nature of well-being can change from one moment to the next. There is a time to laugh and a time to cry, a time to work and a time to play, a time to be awake and a time to sleep. In our waking moments, though, these aims are always for wisdom, compassion, harmony, and creativity. If we seek a single word to describe values such as these, some process theologians use the word "beauty." Thus we can say that God's lure within human life is a lure toward ever increasing beauty.

OBJECTIONS TO PROCESS THEOLOGY

Process theology is controversial for several reasons, most of which pertain to the understanding of God just explained. Three objections are common.

The first is that, for process theologians, God is not all-powerful in a traditional sense. The traditional view has been that once upon a time, before the beginning of creation, God had all the power there was, and that, after creating the universe, God could, if God so chose, intervene in the affairs of the universe in a unilateral way. The paradigmatic example of this unilateral power was that God created the universe out of nothing.

Process theology is controversial because it rejects the idea that there was ever a time when God had all the power and, as a consequence, rejects the idea that God's power is unilateral. Concerning the creation of the universe, process theology proposes, along with Whitehead, that creation is a continuing process, still unfolding, and that there was never a time when only God existed. Thus process theologians propose what is sometimes called a creation-out-of-chaos perspective. Their view is akin to that of the first creation story in Genesis, which suggests that, even at the outset of the universe as we know it, there was a watery chaos over which the Spirit of God brooded, and that God's Spirit evoked or called the heavens and earth into existence from that chaos. From a process perspective, there is wisdom in this point of view. The universe as we know it may (or may not) have begun with a big bang some thirteen billion years ago, prior to which there were no stars, planets, molecules, or even atoms. There was only a dimensionless energy from which a cosmic explosion occurred. But this energy was itself there from the beginning, along with God, and God did not create it out of nothing. Indeed, it may have itself been the result of a contraction of a previous cosmic epoch, in which it took other forms. This energy is the creativity which, for Whitehead, is an ultimate reality. Process theologians further propose that the process of evolution, including its galactic and terrestrial dimensions, is ongoing and will continue forever in one way or another. This is why God does not have, and cannot have, unilateral power. God's power is that of everlasting love, not coercion, evoking various forms of order and novelty from the chaos at hand. To trust in God is not to trust that everything that happens is or even could be a result of God's will. It is to trust that, no matter what happens, there is always hope.

The second reason some people find process theology controversial is that it denies divine foreknowledge. The traditional view has been that all the details of the future are known by God in advance of their occurrence in history. The image is that of God on a mountain, looking down on the past and present and the already determined future, seeing all in a single glance. Process theologians propose, by contrast, that God sees the past and also the present as it is coming into being, but not the future until it occurs. God knows what is possible in the future, but not what is actual until it is actualized by the world. For process theologians, this helps make sense of human freedom and also of the idea that we are called by God. If we were called by God to act in a certain way, but God knew in advance that we would act otherwise, then we would lack the freedom to respond to God's call.

A third reason process theology is controversial is that, by virtue of its rejection of omnipotence and omniscience as traditionally understood, it calls into question the hope and confidence that many Christians feel. This is the hope that at the end of time, whenever that is, "all will be well" through God's power to bring about a state of affairs in which this wellness, however conceived, is realized. For process theologians, this state of affairs cannot occur, because God does not have unilateral power. They add, though, that there are two alternative and valuable ways of understanding what it means to say "all will be well."

One is to recognize that in the receptive side of God—the consequent nature—all the happenings of the universe are gathered into a unified harmony, moment by moment, in which their value is appreciated and affirmed forevermore. In the technical terms of Whiteheadian thought, all things are objectively immortal in the everlasting memory of God. Some add that human beings can have an intuition of this everlasting life in a feeling of peace that they experience in this very life. This is not a peace that excludes tragedy, but rather a peace that includes tragedy in a deeper beauty.

A second way, developed by Marjorie Suchocki and David Ray Griffin, is to affirm that the journey of a human soul or psyche does not end with the death, but that instead there is a continuing journey after death, in which the soul can grow into whatever form of wholeness is optimum for human life as lived in harmony with the rest of creation. On this view, the "wellness" of life does not hinge on a transformation of terrestrial life into a divinely ordained perfection, but rather in the possibility that there is more to life than this life. This view is called subjective immortality. The philosophy of Whitehead avails itself of affirming these two types of immortality: objective immortality in the memory of God and subjective immortality in a continuing journey after death. Should life after death be a fact, the potential of the soul to enter into an ultimate wholeness will depend on the soul's cooperation with

God's will, God's initial aims. Even here, the divine prayer for the soul will need to be answered, or responded to, by the soul itself.

Christians have hoped for life after death for many reasons. The ultimate problem is not death itself. Some deaths can be happy deaths. Moreover, from a process perspective, every moment is a death of sorts: a living and a dying. The problem is incompleteness. It is the fact that so many people and other creatures die without having tasted a wholeness for which they understandably yearn. The hope of the process theologian is that, one way or another, this wholeness can be known in this life or another.

THE FUTURE OF PROCESS THEOLOGY:
PROCESS THEOLOGY IN EAST ASIA

I end this epilogue with some speculations. I have said that the first generation of Christian process theologians were Western. Thanks largely to the work of John Cobb, growing numbers of process theologians now live in other parts of the world. This parallels the fact that today more than sixty percent of Christians live in Asia, Africa, and Latin America. Historians suggest that Christianity is becoming, and in many ways has already become, a post-Western tradition. The future of process theology will lie not only in the West but also, and perhaps even more significantly, in post-Western forms of Christianity. Along the way, process theology will be changed. It will become Asianized, Africanized, and Latin Americanized. What might this look like? I conclude by offering an image of East Asian Christianity as influenced by process ways of thinking.

In East Asia process-oriented Christianities will be shaped by the Bible, but also by Confucianism, Taoism, and Buddhism. These East Asian Christianities will be more than Whiteheadian theologies. For that matter, most Western process theologies are not simply Whiteheadian. Consider the work of John Cobb. He is a Christian in the United Methodist tradition. Methodists often point to four sources of theological insight from which Christians can draw: the Bible, tradition, reason, and experience. Cobb has drawn from each of these sources. He is not simply a Whiteheadian theologian. He is a biblical theologian, a church theologian, an ecological theologian, a liberation theologian, a science-influenced theologian, and a pastoral theologian. He draws upon Whitehead's thought, not as an overriding ideology which dictates all that he thinks, but rather as an intellectually helpful resource for integrating insights from the Bible, tradition, reason, and experience.

The same situation will apply to East Asian process theologies. They will draw from numerous spiritual sources, including the Bible and their own traditions. Whitehead will be one voice among many, not a dominating voice. But insofar as they utilize Whitehead's thought, they will highlight aspects of Whitehead's philosophy that have remained unrecognized or underdeveloped by many Western process theologians. Three examples can make this point.

First, Whitehead's philosophy offers a deeply ecological vision of reality, helping people understand that the Spirit of God is present throughout creation. Nevertheless, with some important exceptions, many process Christian theologians in the West have focused on God's relation to human beings and not on God's presence in hills and rivers. Shaped by nature-centered traditions in Taoism, a process Christian theology emerging in East Asia can be more ecological than Western versions, perhaps helping Western process theologians widen their ecological horizons.

Second, Whitehead's philosophy offers a deeply contemplative vision of reality, helping people understand how they can "feel the feelings" of others and dwell in the Spirit of God, not only by helping others in compasssionate ways, but also by listening to them and by allowing them the space to be themselves. And yet many forms of process theology in the West neglect this listening side of love, focusing more on engaged response to the needs of others.

A process Christian theology emerging in East Asia can partake of the spirit of mindful listening found in Buddhism, helping Christians remember that sometimes the most loving thing we can do for others is not to change them but to listen to them.

Third, Whitehead's philosophy offers a profound emphasis on the role of the body in human life, showing how body and mind are "not one" but also "not two." This opens the door for a respect for ritual as one way in which people can participate in the life of God. Far too many process theologians in the West have neglected ritual as a gateway to God's presence, focusing instead on beliefs and worldviews. A process Christian theology emerging in East Asia—and also in Africa and Latin America in this instance—can help Christians remember that God can be found, not simply in believing in God and acting on the basis of those beliefs, but also in moving with God in ritual and dance. God can also be found in methods of healing that are found in traditional Chinese medicine—practices that build upon a harmony of mind, body, and spirit. Western process theologies have tended to neglect the healing arts as a place where Christianity comes alive, and thus as sacraments in their own right. East Asian Christianities, among others, can help bring God back into healing.

As East Asian Christianities emerge, they will also build upon aspects of Whitehead's thought that have likewise influenced Western process-oriented Christians. For example, a key feature of Whitehead's thought is the idea that a human person is a person-in-community, not an ego-in-isolation. This notion of a person is consistent with Confucian images of the human person. Thus we can well imagine a Confucian Christianity which sees human beings as deeply relational, but which abandons the idea that these relations can or should be hierarchical, as was sometimes the case in classical Confucianism. A Confucian Christianity will then say that dwelling in mutually enhancing relations with other people and with the natural world is itself the heart of discipleship.

In East Asia, of course, as in many other parts of the world, some of the most dynamic forms of Christianity will be in the continued emergence of Evangelical and Pentecostal forms of process thought. Already this is occurring among a handful of evangelical thinkers in the West. Some Evangelicals recognize that the process understanding of God is more consistent with biblical points of view than many classical alternatives, and also that process theology offers promising ways of interpreting Christ and the born-again experience. The same kind of development can occur in Pentecostal traditions, because Christian process theology offers a strong doctrine of the Spirit. It shows how the Spirit can be experienced in silence and in ecstasy, in prophetic action and in music. The value of process theology for Evangelicals and Pentecostals alike is that it can help them make these affirmations while at the same time respecting the wisdom of science, biblical criticism, and other world religions.

In historical Christianity, Christ has been understood in many ways. The majority of Christians have used the word Christ to name (1) the divine Spirit or Logos present throughout the universe, (2) a historical figure—the historical Jesus—in whom that Spirit was embodied, (3) a resurrected savior—the post-Easter Jesus—who is alive in the present and who, upon invitation, can dwell within the heart as a friend and guide. But other Christians have used it in still other ways. Quakers, for example, use the word Christ to name (4) an inner light found in all people that can be a guiding presence in one's life and (5) an atmosphere of love that can be part of a community and felt by others. And liberation theologians have used the word to name (6) the face of the poor and marginalized. Process theologians have typically focused on the first two ways of understanding Christ, but interestingly and importantly, all of these ways can be developed in the ongoing process tradition.

Among Evangelical and Pentecostal Christians, the third way is especially important. Both emphasize the importance of having a relationship with Jesus as one's personal lord and savior. Is this possible? Some would say no, because the universe contains no spirits of any sort. But process theologians can well argue to the contrary. Recall the fact that some them believe that the journey of a soul continues after death. If, in fact, this occurs, there is no reason why Jesus might not be among the souls who thus continues. If this is the case, we can imagine that Jesus' own journey would continue as lived in relationship with those who place their trust in him, with both benefiting. When Christians say "thank you, Jesus," they are not necessarily talking to a dead ancestor. They may well be addressing a living spirit, alive in their hearts, who is a companion along life's way. The cosmology of Whitehead is open to this possibility.

This does not mean that all Christians must have a personal relationship with Christ as resurrected savior. This is one face of Christ, but not the only face. The fourth way is especially important to contemplative Christians. For them, Christ is an inner light and thus a guiding force within one's life. In process theology "inner light" and "guiding force" are initial aims. This way of being connected with Christ can easily be complemented by the fifth way, which is to know Christ in the warmth of loving and compassionate relations with others, including people who are not Christian or who do not believe in Christ. In process theology, Christ would name a certain kind of mood or subjective form that clothes a community when its participants dwell in harmony.

But it is the sixth way—finding Christ in the face of the poor, powerless, and marginalized—that is so important to Christians the world over, even if they also find Christ as inner light or resurrected savior or an atmosphere of love. From a process perspective every moment of experience is a subject for itself but also an object in what comes after it. Every moment is objectively immortal. This means that the very identity of individual humans who lived in the past is not reducible to their lifetime. They can exist in the future too, in the lives of those who come after them. The same applies to Jesus. He was not simply who he was; he is also where he is. Moreover, where Jesus is partly depends on how he is remembered and known by present generations. It is the genius of liberation theologians to say that, if we want to be faithful to Jesus' healing ministry, we must see him, among other places, in the poor, powerless, and marginalized. This does not mean that, as we look into the eyes of a lonely grandmother, or a victim of rape, or a man tortured in prison, or a hungry boy, we must picture Jesus. We have no idea what Jesus looks like. But it does mean that we set our sights on the grandmother and the rape victim and the tortured prisoner and the boy, saying that they do not suffer alone and that we are with them. In a sense, we allow the historical Jesus to be absorbed into their lives, such that in serving them we dwell with him.

One thing that process theology might add, though, is that we also find the face of Christ wherever we find beauty: in the innocence of the child, the mutual care of friends, the intimacy of romance, the wandering of the river, the shining of the stars. Not only in sadness, but also in beauty, we find the salvation of the world. Christians say that we are saved by God's grace. Process theology shows how this grace can be found in this world when, in gentle ways, we are drawn into love.

Notes

1   By "East" I mean people in East Asia, South Asia, and Southeast Asia. Their cultural traditions are quite different, and I beg the reader's indulgence in using such an abstract phrase. By "North" and "South" I mean people in the southern and northern hemispheres. My apologies apply here as well.

2   In many ways he is the founder of process thought, though he neever actually used the phrase "process philosophy," or "process thought," to name his point of view. Thus some people speak of process thought as Whiteheadian thought.

3   Some well-known process philosophers and theologians in this first generation of process thought include Charles Hartshorne, Henry Nelson Weiman, Bernard Meland, and John B. Cobb, Jr. Some of these thinkers are still very active today and still adding new chapters, as are many of their students: David Ray Griffin and Marjorie Suchocki, for example.

4 To make this point, some people speak of process thought as
   international process thought. A global network has been estab-
   lished—the International Process Network—to help keep participants in communication. Learn more at: http://processnetwork.
   net.

5 In the West, the phrase originates from an essay by John Donne
   (1572–1631), Meditation XVII.

6 For Whiteheadian readers, I am using the word "patterns" to
   refer to what Whitehead calls eternal objects of the objective
   and subjective species that have been periodically and habitually
   ingressed in the affairs of the universe (laws of nature) and
   human life (customs of society). Eternal objects of the objective
   species pertain to relations of extension and are the domain of
   the physical sciences and mathematics. Eternal objects of the
   subjective species pertain to subjective form—feelings of pleasure
   and pain, appreciation and depreciation, suffering and joy—and
   are the domain of human (and nonhuman animal) custom. In
   suggesting that patterns can change, I am referring to the idea that
   the laws of nature can change with different cosmic epochs, and
   that human and nonhuman customs are evolving over time, such
   that social traditions can incorporate aspects of other cultures into
   their own ongoing life-history, thus changing their own customs.
   Globalization is very much a context of the latter.

7 For Whiteheadians, I use the term intersubjectivity to refer to
   the fact that every moment of experience begins with an act of
   feeling the feelings of others, and also to the fact that, through
   what Whitehead calls hybrid physical prehensions, it is possible
   that humans can feel the feelings of other people in a way not
   unlike that in which they feel the feelings of their own past
   personal experiences. Technically speaking, of course, two people
   cannot apprehend the immediate subjective states of others at the
   same time; they can only feel the subjective states from the past.
   However, in ordinary human experience, humans often sense
   that they are attuned to the moods and emotions of others in the
   present, and a Whiteheadian approach must accommodate this

fact if it is to be adequate to experience. The term intersubjectivity refers to such mutuality.

8   By "cosmology," I mean a scientifically informed vision of the universe.

9   Process thinkers played small but important roles in helping bring the Earth Charter into existence, as part of a working group. The Earth Charter is an authoritative synthesis of values, principles, and aspirations that are widely shared by growing numbers of people, in all regions of the world. The principles of the Earth Charter reflect extensive international consultations conducted over a period of many years. These principles are also based upon contemporary science, international law, and the insights of philosophy and religion. Successive drafts of the Earth Charter were circulated around the world for comments and debate by nongovernmental organizations, community groups, professional societies, and international experts in many fields. Learn more at: www.earthcharter.org.

10   See: http://www.minessence.net/eZine/eZine21.aspx.

11   Complementary to healthy consumption is what we might call creative frugality. Creative frugality lies in taking care of material possessions, utilizing them rather than discarding them, and appreciating them. Such frugality involves a healthy respect for material things in life, and in this sense it is deeply materialistic. But its materialism is free rather than controlled by external factors, and it is frugal rather than greedy. In the English language the word "frugal" can mean stingy and un-generous, or it can mean careful and care-filled. Creative frugality is careful and care-filled. It does not escape the material world for a more ethereal world. Instead it celebrates the blessings of materiality. But it is not at all stingy. Indeed, people who consume in creatively frugal ways are often more generous than people who are absorbed in conspicuous consumption. But creative frugality has a joyful and reverential quality to it, because it actually appreciates the material dimensions of life and does not want to be wasteful. This joy is obstructed by consumerism, which makes a god of

consumption itself.

12   The United Nations estimates that 1.2 billion people live on less than $1 a day and almost 3 billion on less than $2 a day. 110 million primary school age children are out of school; 31 million people are infected with HIV/AIDS. The poor people of our world do not need to consume less; they need to consume more. (*Editor's Note:* Since 2015, the World Bank has defined extreme poverty as living on less than $1.90 a day. The definition also changed to include multidimensional factors (living standards, education, and healthcare). In 107 developing countries, 1.3 billion people are multidimensionally poor, according to a (pre-COVID-19) 2020 report by the U.N. Development Program. The World Bank estimates that the COVID-19 pandemic is likely to push between 88 and 115 million people into extreme poverty in 2020, setting back poverty reduction by around three years.

13   See Ian Barbour, *Nature, Human Nature, and God.* Philadelphia: Fortress Press, 2000, 66–67.

14   Barbour, *Nature, Human Nature, and God,* 66–67.

LIST OF ABBREVIATIONS

AI   *Adventures of Ideas.* 1933. New York: Free Press, 1967.

MT   *Modes of Thought.* 1938. New York: Free Press, 1968.

PR   *Process and Reality.* 1929. Corrected Edition. Ed. David Ray Griffin and Donald W. Sherburne. New York: Free Press, 1978.

SMW   *Science and the Modern World.* 1925. New York: Free Press, 1967.

Made in the USA
Middletown, DE
13 November 2022

14906326R00080